OBJECT-ORIENTED DATABASES
Applications in Software Engineering

THE McGRAW-HILL
INTERNATIONAL SERIES IN SOFTWARE ENGINEERING

Consulting Editor

Professor D Ince
The Open University

Other titles

Portable Modula-2 Programming – Woodman, Griffiths, Souter and Davies
Software Engineering: Analysis and Design – Easteal and Davies
SSADM: A Practical Approach – Ashworth and Goodland
Introduction to Compiling Techniques: A First Course Using ANSI C, LEX and YACC – Bennett
Practical Formal Methods With VDM – Andrews and Ince
An Introduction to Program Design – Sargent
Expert Database Systems: A Gentle Introduction – Beynon-Davies

in

OBJECT-ORIENTED DATABASES
Applications in
Software Engineering

Alan W. Brown
Lecturer at the Institute of Software Engineering
Carnegie–Mellon University

McGRAW-HILL BOOK COMPANY

London · New York · St Louis · San Francisco · Auckland · Bogotá
Caracas · Hamburg · Lisbon · Madrid · Mexico · Milan · Montreal
New Delhi · Panama · Paris · San Juan · São Paulo · Singapore
Sydney · Tokyo · Toronto

Published by
McGRAW-HILL Book Company Europe
SHOPPENHANGERS ROAD · MAIDENHEAD · BERKSHIRE SL6 2QL · ENGLAND
TELEPHONE: 0628 23432
FAX: 0628 770224

British Library Cataloguing in Publication Data
Brown, Alan W.
  Object-oriented databases: their applications to software
  engineering. – (The McGraw-Hill international series in
  software engineering)
  1. Databases
  I. Title
005.74

ISBN 0-07-707247-2

Library of Congress Cataloging-in-Publication Data
Brown, Alan W.
  Object-oriented databases and their applications to software
  engineering/Alan W. Brown.
  p. cm. – (The McGraw-Hill international series in software
  engineering)
  Includes bibliographical references and index.
  ISBN 0-07-707247-2
  1. Object-oriented data bases.   2. Software engineering.
  I. Title.   II. Series.
QA76.9.D3B77   1991
005.75–dc20   90-48238 CIP

234 PB 9321

Typeset by the author

and printed and bound in Great Britain by Page Bros, Norwich

CONTENTS

PREFACE

In the short history of computer science there have been a number of important concepts which have appeared to alter fundamentally current thinking and perceptions. Typically the life-cycle of these mini-revolutions progresses something like this: one or two eminent computer scientists produce seminal papers concerning the new concept, perhaps accompanied by support tools (e.g. a language, a methodology, an application system, or a new machine architecture). After some preliminary discussion of this work in the literature and at relevant conferences, there is a massive take-up of the new ideas resulting in a plethora of systems claiming to have adopted the new approach. Almost as soon as this widespread acceptance reaches fever pitch, however, a few dissenting voices are heard questioning the new approach. Usually these non-believers have looked at a number of the systems which claim to have adopted the new concept, only to find that the concept has been applied very differently in each case. As Meyer (1988) notes, they normally raise three basic objections:

1. The new concept is just a new name for something we already do.

2. The new concept is trivial, and of no real value.

3. The new concept is unworkable for their particular application area.

It then becomes clear that the original concept has not been fully appreciated by many of its converts, resulting in many conflicting theories and proposals as to the components of the concept, its interpretation, and in particular its application. A long period of claim and counter-claim often ensues, usually leading to the creation of numerous factions with different interpretations of the same underlying concept.

A number of well-known examples illustrate the outline above: structured programming, expert systems, reduced instruction set computers (RISC machines), relational databases, and functional programming can all be said to fall into this pattern.

It now appears that a new concept is following this life-cycle, perhaps more spectacularly than any of the other examples given: the *object-oriented approach*. Following its conception in the early eighties, it seems that object-orientation is an attribute which every language, system, tool, and application must have.

To a large extent this position was correctly predicted in 1982 by Tim Rentsch:

> My guess is that object-oriented programming will be in the 1980's what structured programming was in the 1970's. Everyone will be in favor of it. Every manufacturer will promote his products as supporting it. Every manager will pay lip service to it. Every programmer will practice it (differently).
> And no-one will know just what it is!

In fact, the object-oriented concept has been even more pervasive than Rentsch anticipated. The table below gives examples of areas of computer science which have adopted the object-oriented concept in some form.

Computing field	Examples
Programming languages	Simula, Smalltalk, C++
User interfaces	Mac, PM
Design methods	HOOD, Booch
Operating systems	Mach, Eden, Clouds
Hardware architecture	Recursiv

It can be seen that in addition to programming languages, user interfaces, software design methods, operating systems, and even computer architectures have been described as object-oriented.

The object-oriented concept has recently infected the database community to the extent that conferences, workshops, and tutorials are beginning to be aimed exclusively at the new area of *object-oriented databases*. However, even as the first object-oriented database products are appearing in the market-place, there remains great confusion as to the characteristics, advantages, limitations, and applications of object-oriented database technology. This book addresses these issues by analysing the characteristics common to object-oriented systems and applications, and reviews a number of database systems which embody many of those concepts.

It is important to recognize that object-oriented database systems have been developed largely as a response to the data management requirements of computer-aided design applications. To highlight the effects this has had on the development of object-oriented database technology, the book is based around a particular application area which provides a context in which the technology can be evaluated. Of the many possible application areas within the broader computer-aided design field, in this book we shall concentrate on the computer-aided design of software itself, often referred to as *computer-aided software engineering (CASE)* or *integrated project support environments (IPSEs)*. It is envisaged, however, that the discussion would remain largely unchanged if a different computer-aided design activity were used instead (for example, VLSI circuit design, or mechanical component design).

Two questions arise in connection with the subject matter of this book:

1. Is it still too soon after the start of real interest in object-oriented databases to produce a book describing the characteristics of this technology?

2. What can the reader expect to learn from working through this book ?

The answers to both of these questions are closely related: the aim of this book is to provide no more than a snapshot of current thinking in the area of object-oriented databases. Certainly it is the author's belief that the next few years will see widespread dissemination of the object-oriented approach, with the result that new and important insights into the technology will be gained. These in turn will lead to extensive developments in the approach and its technology. Hence, this book is not intended as *the* definitive description of this area. However, the more modest aims of this book are to provide the reader with a comprehensive and cogent introduction to the motivation for object-oriented database systems, to provide an overview of the issues as they are presently perceived, and thus to enable the reader to follow, understand, and perhaps influence the future development of the object-oriented approach to database systems.

Intended Audience

This book is an introduction to object-oriented database systems, with emphasis on their use as an enabling technology for supporting large-scale software development. Hence, the primary intended audience for this book encompasses a wide range of people from both the academic and industrial communities who are currently working in:

1. the database field, and are interested to discover how object-oriented techniques are being applied to the database systems area; or

2. the software engineering field, and wish to learn about object-oriented databases and their use as the basis for computer-aided support of software

development activities.

As a result, the book may be particularly appropriate as a text for advanced undergraduate courses in database systems, or in software engineering. In addition, the extensive bibliography provided in this book should prove valuable to the growing number of postgraduate students working in the area of object-oriented database systems.

The industrial research and development community is also turning its attention towards object-oriented systems. This book provides an introduction to the concepts involved, and an extensive bibliography to point the way for future work in this area.

Organization of the Book

In the remainder of this book we examine in more detail the concept of object-oriented databases and their use in integrated project support environments. In particular, the book is split into two self-contained parts. The first part provides an introduction to object-oriented databases, and particularly their application to software engineering. This first part is organized as follows:

- Chapter 1 provides general motivation for the work on object-oriented database systems. It concentrates on design applications such as software development support as a major catalyst for that work. The problems in applying existing database technology to those design applications are briefly reviewed.

- Chapter 2 examines the main components of the object-oriented approach, particularly the general characteristics found in current programming language implementations of the object-oriented model.

- Chapter 3 reviews some of the background work which has been taking place within the database field leading to the current interest in object-orientation within database systems. This leads on to a discussion on the use of the term 'object-oriented' as it applies specifically to database systems.

- Chapter 4 provides a review of a number of selected implementations of object-oriented databases. This provides a useful indication of the current state of the art in this field. In conclusion, a number of interesting points of comparison are examined.

- Chapter 5 discusses the use of object-oriented databases as they apply specifically to IPSEs. The characteristics of an object-oriented database are evaluated against a set of IPSE data management requirements. Then, a number of interesting systems are reviewed with regard to their use of object-oriented database technology for supporting software design. From this work, an outline methodology for IPSE development is constructed.

- Chapter 6 provides a summary of the main characteristics of the object-oriented approach to database systems, looks at some of the possible limitations of this approach, and speculates on the possible future importance of object-oriented database technology.

The second part of the book consists of a single chapter containing an extensive bibliography on object-oriented database systems. The references are organized into a number of broad categories, and for each category a brief review of some of the most informative references has been provided. This part of the book will be invaluable as a source of further reading for those who wish to find out more about object-oriented databases and their applications.

Acknowledgements

I am indebted to a number of people for their help and assistance during the writing of this book, and it is my privilege to be able to acknowledge their contributions:

- Members of the Department of Computer Science at York who provided comments and feedback on early drafts of this book. The content and form of the book has been greatly enhanced by their work. My thanks to Derek Bridge, Peter Hitchcock, John McDermid, and Martin Atkins who have been particularly helpful in this regard.

- The (anonymous) referees who provided some very helpful and constructive comments on an early draft of the book.

- Chris Higgins for his invaluable assistance in formatting the text.

In addition, some of the early work for this book was carried out during a Short-Term Fellowship with British Telecom Research Laboratories. My thanks to all at RT3131 for their help in carrying out that work.

Finally, biggest thanks of all go to Moira West for her help and assistance in reading, questioning, criticizing, and scribbling on earlier drafts of this book. Her assistance has not only improved the final form of the book, it also made the process of writing it much more fun.

Alan W. Brown
Department of Computer Science
University of York
November 1990

LIST OF TRADEMARKS

UNIX is a trademark of AT&T Bell Laboratories

Smalltalk is a trademark of the Xerox Corporation

Object-SQL is a trademark of Oracle Corporation UK Ltd

GemStone is a registered trademark of Servio Logic Development Corporation

OPAL is a trademark of Servio Logic Development Corporation

ONTOS is a trademark of Ontologic Inc.

Oracle is a registered trademark of the Oracle Corporation UK Ltd

Software BackPlane is a trademark of Atherton Technology

Software through Pictures is a trademark of IDE

DEC is a trademark of the Digital Equipment Corporation

VAX is a trademark of the Digital Equipment Corporation

Excelerator is a trademark of Index Technology

Ada is a trademark of the US Government (AJPO)

DesignAid and CASE 2000 are trademarks of NASTEC Corporation

X Windows is a trademark of Massachusetts Institute of Technology

Part I

An Introduction to Object-oriented Databases

MOTIVATION

Throughout the past two decades there has been an unprecedented increase in the application of computer technology. We can identify three important reasons for this:

1. A dramatic increase in computing power. Computer main memories are now measured in millions of bytes, secondary memories in billions of bytes, and CPU speeds in millions of instructions executed per second.

2. A continuing fall in the real cost of computing hardware. The availability of powerful microcomputers at low cost makes computing technology available to every organization, and even many individuals.

3. A growing acceptance of computerization within the business community, and a widening of application areas which directly employ computers.

This rapid increase in computing use has had a number of important consequences. In particular, the demand for computer software has not been met by the software producers (the so-called 'software crisis'), and furthermore the complexity of software being produced is on the increase. It is not particularly unusual to hear of large-scale software development projects producing in excess of a million lines of code as a deliverable for a large data-processing application, or real-time embedded system (Rowland and Welsch, 1983; Glass, 1982).

Clearly, as software development projects reach this scale, the problems of software production become significant. Producing such systems within budget and on time is problem enough. Designing a system so that it can easily evolve as the operating environment changes, as user requirements are modified, and as errors (which inevitably occur in such large systems) come to light, make this an even more difficult task. We can identify two distinct strands to this problem.

Firstly, the methods which are employed within the different phases of the life of a software product must be closely examined. Techniques must be developed which help in unravelling the complexity of software system design and development, covering the varied tasks of requirements capture, system design, software implementation, system testing and post-operational maintenance. A great deal of work has been carried out over the past decade aimed at defining methods, languages and notations which can be used to help produce an understandable model of a complex real-world situation.

Secondly, bitter experience has shown that producing succinct but individual solutions to each of the problems of software development does not automatically imply that the problems of software production have been solved. There are a whole series of problems which arise simply because developing a large software system inevitably involves a large group of people, working over a long period of time, and producing a vast amount of information (requirements documents, system designs, production schedules, test data reports, and so on). Post-mortems from a number of large software projects have revealed that this second category of problems had as much influence on the success or failure of the project as the technical issues which are often wrongly thought of as the critical aspect (Rowland and Welsch, 1983; Brooks, 1975).

Hence, developing large, complex software systems not only requires that significant *technical* problems are overcome, it also requires many *managerial* issues to be addressed: the organization, monitoring, and control of the project's development to ensure its continued progress.

Typically, software projects are supported by some form of computerized development environment with automated tools to help with the application and use of a particular method, language, or notation. In many cases this consists of no more than the file store of the computer's host operating system as a persistent data repository, with some *ad hoc* collection of software tools to help with some of the development tasks. For many software developers a text editor, programming language compiler, and object code debugger form their everyday software development environment. Systems analysts may additionally have tools which help automate the construction of designs in a particular structured design notation.

Helpful as these individual tools are, there are a number of important aspects of software development which receive very little support from development environments formed from loose collections of individual tools. These include:

- *Management visibility.*   A major problem associated with large system development is that the current state of the project must be continually reviewed to ensure its progress. It is very difficult to maintain management control over a project when individual developers use disparate tools which produce information in different formats and bury it within files.

- *Developer communication.* A software developer rarely works in isolation. One developer will rely on the results of another developer's work, and must constrain what he/she does to meet the requirements of yet another developer's needs.

- *Information sharing.* The strong relationships that exist between different phases of the software development life-cycle imply that common interfaces must be defined between different pieces of work. For example, the systems analyst must rely on the requirements document being correct and up to date. Whenever changes to the requirements are necessary, the information must be shared between the systems analyst and the requirements analyst.

The need for a more supportive environment for software development has long been recognized. One of the most important approaches currently being investigated is the development of an infrastructure of common services which can be used as the basis of a software development environment. Such environments are called *integrated project support environments (IPSEs).*[1]

1.1 INTEGRATED PROJECT SUPPORT ENVIRONMENTS

By way of an informal definition of an IPSE it is useful to examine each of the words of this phrase and interpret its meaning in this context.

- *Integrated.* The support provided by an IPSE will cover a wide range of activities. It is important that such support is consistent, individual tools work together, and that information is shared throughout software development.

- *Project.* An IPSE must help in more than just the software programming tasks. More specifically, software development includes requirements definition, design, testing, maintenance, and so on. An IPSE must address itself to many (if not all) of these activities.

- *Support.* An IPSE must provide as much support for the development process as possible. At a simple level this may imply that an IPSE provides mechanisms for controlling data integrity, thus preventing the IPSE from many kinds of errors. In more advanced IPSEs, support may include the use of knowledge-based techniques to control and direct user actions more closely.

- *Environment.* IPSE support must address managerial aspects (visibility, planning, resource allocation, and so on) as well as the technical. In this way the IPSE is a complete environment for software development.

---

[1] Other alternative terms which are commonly used include software engineering environment (SEE) and computer-assisted software engineering (CASE) environment. These terms are treated as being synonymous for the purposes of this discussion.

The past decade has seen a great deal of work investigating the functionality required from systems aimed at supporting the process of large-scale software development. The Stoneman report (Buxton, 1980) is perhaps the key landmark of the early work in this area.

1.1.1   The Stoneman model

The architecture of an IPSE was initially guided by work carried out to define requirements for an Ada programming support environment (APSE), reported in the Stoneman document (Buxton, 1980). Here, the need for automated support for the development of large Ada programs led to the definition of a set of requirements outlining the basic architectural components of an APSE. To summarize, the basis of any APSE must be a database which records data items and their relationships in a structured and accessible form. The database provides a set of core services for tools that communicate through this structured data repository. A kernel Ada programming support environment (KAPSE) is then defined as the database together with communication and run-time support to allow Ada programs to be executed. With the addition of a minimal set of tools to support the creation and maintenance of Ada programs, a minimal Ada programming support environment (MAPSE) results. Finally, a complete Ada programming support environment (APSE) is constructed by extending the MAPSE to provide support for different programming methodologies and techniques. This architecture is illustrated in Fig. 1.1.

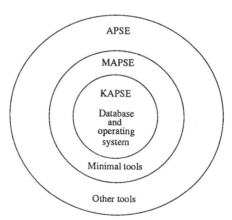

Figure 1.1   Basic architecture of an APSE

An important feature of the architecture is the interface between the KAPSE and MAPSE. This interface provides access to the set of services provided by the KAPSE for the tools implemented as part of the MAPSE and APSE. In this sense it is equivalent to what is often called a public tool interface (PTI) (Lyons, 1986).

While the approach and architecture advocated in the Stoneman report have gained a wide measure of acceptance over the last few years, it is clear that the coarse granularity of the layers within the architecture have led to a great deal of confusion. The simple division into KAPSE tools and MAPSE tools means that the relationships which exist between services within each of these layers are not made explicit in the architecture. We can more effectively review the functionality which is commonly provided in an IPSE system by considering an IPSE as a set of available services.

1.1.2   IPSE services

We can roughly divide the support provided by an IPSE system into one of a small set of services. Different IPSE systems may use different mechanisms and may offer varying levels of support for each service we will identify, but our description will at least provide a reasonably implementation-independent description of an IPSE. It is important to note, however, that the architecture of individual IPSE systems will determine how these services are organized internally, and also which services can be accessed externally by the end user. For example, one IPSE system may choose to allow an end user to manipulate the system directly through operators provided by the operating system, while another may choose to insulate the user totally from that level of service so that an end user only accesses operating system services indirectly through other (higher level) services (e.g. through database operations).

A common source of confusion is the role of what are traditionally called 'software tools'. When an IPSE system is designed, a choice is made as to which services are to be provided as integral to the IPSE system, and which must be later added by IPSE end users. The rationale behind the choice often lies in a trade-off between how useful and pervasive the service will be to the software development process, measured against its consequent effect on the efficiency and performance of the IPSE system as a whole. Hence, different IPSE designers have made different choices as to those services which are provided as part of the IPSE infrastructure itself, and those which must be added to the IPSE through tool building. One example is the set of version control facilities that are provided in an IPSE. Early IPSE systems relied on particular tools to provide such services (such as SCCS (Feldman, 1979) and RCS (Tichy, 1982)) while later systems have a basic set of version services built-in (Leblang and Chase, 1984).

We shall identify seven main classes of IPSE service which may be provided.

The hardware services

The lowest level of service provided will be at the hardware level. While it is unlikely that end users of an IPSE system will be given direct access to operators at this level, it is important to recognize that the hardware services will be used internally within the IPSE. For example, it is probable that IPSE systems will be distributed over homogeneous or heterogeneous hardware platforms. Much of the internal work of the IPSE will then be concerned with making sure the hardware platform performs as a single integrated system.

The operating system services

The minimum IPSE system consists of a set of operating system services on top of which end users can build development tools. In many ways a simple operating system environment can be considered as a first generation IPSE system (Morgan, 1987).

The operators provided at this level will allow interaction with a file system for persistent data storage, low-level control of user processes, and a shell for constraining execution of user programs.

The data control services

A second generation of IPSE system (Morgan, 1987) augments the operating system services with enhanced data storage and control facilities. Typically this means that a database system is provided which offers general qualities of improved data sharing mechanisms, finer grained control of data relationships, generalized data querying, and more sophisticated logging, security, and recovery services.

As the basis of IPSE support for software development applications is to provide control for the large and complex body of data generated throughout a software project, these services can be considered to be the basic mechanisms of an IPSE system.

The information control services

Capturing the semantics of software development applications requires more active support to be provided by the IPSE system. The next level of services augments the database with rule and inferencing mechanisms to provide more of a knowledge base of information rather than a static database of facts.

Through these mechanisms it should be possible to capture the complex relationships and dependencies which exist in software development more adequately. In particular, triggers and alerters can be attached to data to fire off procedures automatically when changes are made to data items.

The process control services

So far the services outlined have been very general data storage and data management mechanisms. An additional requirement is for special facilities appropriate to software development applications. In particular, key services to software support are those for version control and configuration management. These must be provided as an integral part of the IPSE system.

Additionally, modelling of the software development process requires that the IPSE system provides the ability not only to represent the usual data items such as documents and programs, but also to model the users who produce these data items, the roles which users may assume, and the high-level tasks which produce the data items. These basic services allow not only the software product, but also the development process itself to be represented and controlled in the IPSE.

The method control services

Making use of the data storage mechanisms provided, tools will cooperate within an organizational framework which supports a particular method of system development. It is at this point that particular methods which the IPSE system supports are bound into the environment. Typically these services will support diagrammatic methods such as data flow diagrams, structure diagrams, Jackson Structured Design (JSD) (Sutcliffe, 1988), MASCOT (Bate, 1986), and so on, and direct the way in which information is shared between these methods.

The project control services

Finally, for a particular IPSE system the services provided will be tailored towards the needs of an individual organization. This might include the application of management constraints, organizational guidelines, reporting structure, and company standards.

While such constraints may be enforced by the way in which the other services have been customized and used, these constraints also imply a restriction or tailoring of the services available to the end users. So, while the functionality of the IPSE system may not be extended, it will certainly be affected.

1.2 SOFTWARE DEVELOPMENT IS A DATABASE APPLICATION

In recent years much attention has focused on the requirements of software development environments. It has been found that a key requirement for providing effective support is the *integration* that is provided within the software development environment. The concept of integration can manifest itself in a number of different ways within the development environment, and it is common to interpret integration in one or more of the following ways:

- Each tool has the same set of constructs at the user interface. Hence, this standardizes the way in which users interact with tools, simplifying the use of a set of tools.

- The environment has been constructed to support a single software development methodology. For example, the Perspective system (Brown, 1989) was designed for supporting the development of real-time embedded avionics software systems. It provides a tool for capturing system requirements in the CORE notation (Mullery, 1979) and semi-automatically generates software to implement requirements in an extended form of the Pascal programming language. In addition, host-target debugging tools are provided for the object code this language produces. The result is a development environment which is well integrated in the sense that the tools work together with a common understanding of the software development life-cycle supported.

- To allow tools to share data, a common data format can be defined. The most obvious example of this is the UNIX development environment (Kernighan and Mashey, 1979) in which all data is assumed to be in the form of a simple stream of bytes. Tools may be combined very easily as a data consumer tool (e.g. a printer driver) can expect the output from a data producer (e.g. a text processor) to arrive in a predefined form.

- The environment may be aimed at a single programming language. A number of programming support environments have been constructed which provide very strong support for software developed in a particular language (Cheatham, 1981). These environments can provide structured editors, optimizing compilers, and symbolic debuggers for the chosen language. A generalization of this approach is to provide tool-generating tools for a given language syntax. For example, tools are available to generate a lexical analyser and parser from a definition of the syntax of the given language. This approach has been enhanced to allow a complete suite of tools to be generated for a given language definition (Teitelbaum and Reps, 1981).

While all of the above provide interpretations of the term 'integrated' with respect to a software development environment, we can also adopt a somewhat more general notion of this term, based on viewing software development as a data processing activity. In particular, a recognized way of providing this integration is through building support tools around a shared data storage facility. Such a facility reduces the need for maintaining multiple copies of the same data, provides a general language for data definition and manipulation, enforces some measure of consistency within the data, is self-describing (allowing you to query the repository to find out what kind of data it contains), and includes some mechanisms for controlled data sharing. These are the facilities which are typically provided by existing *database management systems (DBMS)*.

The principle advantage of DBMSs are that they provide (logically) centralized control of the users' operational data (Date, 1986). That is, the data which is of interest is no longer embedded in, and distributed among the applications which use the data. Instead it is maintained as an independent resource with controlled redundancy and sharing. While the general advantages of the database approach to maintaining large amounts of data have been described often (Date, 1986; Brown, 1989), it is useful to examine the particular advantages of using a database for maintaining software development data. We can illustrate these advantages with a simple example.

1.2.1   An example

Consider the use of a simple database system to record information about a software project. Figure 1.2 shows an entity–relationship model of the data to be represented.

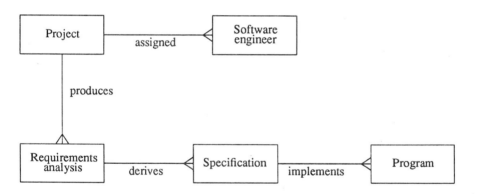

Figure 1.2   An example software development schema

Boxes depict entity types, and arcs between boxes represent relationships between entity types. The information recorded in this schema can be interpreted as follows: information is recorded about different software projects, each of which is assigned a number of software engineers. A software engineer works on only one project at a time. A project produces a number of requirements analysis reports, each of which may in turn derive many specification documents. Finally, each specification document may itself be implemented as a number of programs.[1]

Even this simple schema can illustrate a number of important advantages of capturing such information in a database system. In particular, it is useful to consider each of the different classes of user of this information. We shall examine three such classes: the project manager, the software engineer, and the quality assurance engineer.

The project manager

Using a database approach, it is possible to explicitly represent information relating to project personnel and the projects to which they are assigned. Using a general query language the project manager can analyse the data to find the current state of each of the projects (e.g. which specifications have been implemented and tested) and hence use the information in decision-making. For example, when planning a new project, the allocation of resources on current projects can be analysed and decisions made based on this information.

The software engineer

A software engineer may be involved in producing any of the requirement reports, specification documents, or programs. However, there is a clear requirement that information is shared between engineers. For example, a program implementor writes the program with respect to the current program specification document, and therefore must be able to access the appropriate specification. Such constraints between software engineers must be made explicit and must be controlled to ensure that confusion between developers is reduced.

The quality assurance engineer

An important role within a project is assumed by quality assurance engineers. They are responsible for testing and validating each of the documents and programs generated during a project. In particular they check that each piece of work has been performed according to a set of defined standards, and has reached a specified level of quality. The information captured within the database schema can be used as the basis for their work. For example, they must check that software engineers have used the correct specification document when writing their code, and that the specification document in turn was derived from the appropriate requirements analysis report. Much of the information they need can be captured in the database schema.

---

[1]While it is clear that this example is a gross simplification of the real-world situation, we use it here simply to illustrate a number of points raised in the text—*not* as an example of a realistic schema for a software project!

1.2.2   Summary

The important point which has been made by the above example is that *database support is an essential component of any environment which supports large-scale software development.* In fact, we can be more emphatic than that and say that it is the underlying database component of an IPSE which will determine the overall effectiveness of any such environment.

1.3   THE PROBLEMS OF APPLYING EXISTING DATABASE TECHNOLOGY

While the general principle of applying the database approach to recording software development data is clear, it is important to recognize that database development has mainly been geared towards commercial applications, holding information such as personnel details and bank records. This has led to the development of techniques which make databases highly efficient in commercial environments, but they are not necessarily so suitable for other application areas whose characteristics differ from these environments. Where conventional database systems have been used in software development environments, it has been found that the mechanisms and services of the database system are not particularly appropriate for the software development application. As many people have noted (Bernstein and Lomet, 1987; Brown, 1989), the requirements for a software engineering database are significantly different from those of existing commercial database systems. Table 1.1 is a summary of the main differences between the requirements for a commercial database, and those of a database designed specifically to record software engineering data.

We can gain some appreciation of the different requirements of using a database system for recording software development data by considering the characteristics of a typical database interaction.

For example, when a software engineer is required to make an update to a program module, the following actions may take place. First, having located the original program module within the database, some way of obtaining exclusive access to that module is required. To perform the changes to the module the software engineer may well require access to a large number of other data items, including the original specification of the program module, the bug report which necessitated this change, related modules which provide input to this faulty module, details of previous test results, and so on. Depending upon the changes required, it may take anything up to a number of weeks to complete the amendments, to test the module, and finally to obtain approval from the quality assurance engineers that the module can be released for use.

Table 1.1   Comparison of commercial and software engineering databases

Commercial database	*Software engineering database*
Most information is static and can be described *a priori*, so the schema is also static and compiled.	Continuous evolution of information — data about the environment itself (tools, methods, etc.) and the products being developed.
Update to the schema is infrequent, and controlled by a group of database administrators.	Change to the schema is expected and frequent. Many users will need to change the schema.
Data stored is atomic and fixed length (e.g. strings and numbers).	Data stored is atomic, but also structured. Could be graphical data, design documents, programs, and so on. Also, data items may be large and complex, and of variable length.
Small number of entity types, with large number of instances of each type. Often only simple, fixed relationships between entity types exist.	Many entity types, with fewer instances of each type. Complex relationships may exist between entity types, and new relationships may be created.
Initially loaded with a large amount of data. Slow, constant rate of data growth.	Less data initially loaded. Rapid growth of database (both of structure and contents), which slows down after completion of design phase.
Single-valued data items, which are updated in place.	Versions of data items are vital. Dependence on versions, and relationships between versions must be explicitly recorded.
Transactions are short, atomic, and can be used as the basis for concurrent data access.	Long-lived transactions (minutes, or hours) which may leave the database inconsistent for long periods. Cannot be conveniently used as locking units.

With a traditional database system the mechanisms provided to support such an example are severely limited. In particular, we can identify at least three difficulties with the above scenario.

1. Exclusive access to large amounts of data in the database will require it to be made inaccessible to others through the database locking mechanism. In many cases this prevents such data even being read by other users for the whole of the database interaction. If we consider the above scenario as a single (extended) database interaction, the lock may need to be maintained for many days.

2. Maintenance of complex relationships between data items is more difficult to support in a traditional database system. In particular, even with this simplified example, we can begin to have some appreciation of the complexity of the relationships which commonly exist in software engineering. Of crucial importance is the notion of a version relationship between two data items. While simplified version mechanisms can be modelled in a traditional database system (Huff, 1981), the importance of versions and configurations to software development applications leads to a number of ramifications with regard to database storage and performance.

3. There are complex integrity constraints that must be enforced. For instance, we may want to constrain software engineers to produce code according to the company's defined guidelines and procedures. It is difficult to envisage how the traditional database constraint mechanisms can be extended to support this sort of requirement.

1.4   APPROACHES TO PROVIDING SOFTWARE DEVELOPMENT DATABASES

There are two possible approaches to dealing with the inadequacies of commercial database systems.

1. A commercial database system is used with a further layer of software providing additional database services which replace or augment the implemented database facilities. For example, the existing locking mechanisms may be replaced by new transaction mechanisms which support extended periods of database interaction. In addition, support for multiple versions of database objects may be added.

2. A commercial database system is *not* used. Rather, a new set of data management services is produced 'in-house'. These services are tuned to the requirements of the support environment.

Each of these alternatives has its advantages and disadvantages. While the first approach avoids the need to write many of the database facilities from scratch, it can still involve a very significant amount of work. Indeed, many of the mechanisms are in fact 'excess baggage' and may significantly impair overall performance. Also, with the majority of existing database systems it is very difficult to take advantage of some of the services provided while overriding others. Not only are the systems closed to such attempts to divide up their functionality, but it may also take a great deal of effort to add new services in a seamless and integrated fashion.

The second approach, however, is undertaken in the light that existing commercial database systems represent many years of production effort. It is a major undertaking to design and implement a new database system. In its favour, of course, is the fact that the facilities provided by such a bespoke system should be well matched with the requirements of the application, significantly improving overall system performance.

The last few years, however, have seen a number of major research efforts directed at the problems of database support for engineering applications. Not only have the requirements and design characteristics of engineering databases been debated, but also the first attempts have been made at designing and implementing general database systems specifically for these applications. As can be expected, many different solutions have been proposed. What is quite unexpected is the significant overlap in the solutions adopted. They almost all suggest some form of *object-oriented database system* as providing the most promising way forward.

The rest of this book examines the background to, and characteristics of, object-oriented database systems, concluding with an examination of their use in supporting large-scale software development.

1.5   ENGINEERING DESIGN DATABASES

While this book concentrates exclusively on software engineering applications as the driving force for object-oriented database systems, it is worth noting that the task of software development shares a number of common characteristics with other engineering design activities. Most notably, the field of engineering design can be said to encompass software engineering design, computer-aided design (CAD), computer-aided engineering (CAE), computer-aided manufacturing (CAM), and (to a lesser extent) office information systems (OIS).

A number of studies have examined the data management requirements of these activities, and a large measure of overlap has been found (Morgan, 1986; Katz, 1986; Buchmann, 1984; Brown, 1988). For example, in storing information about very large scale integration (VLSI) designs of hardware components in a CAD system the complex, hierarchical nature of VLSI components is immediately evident. Similarly the need for recording multiple versions of a particular design is obvious.

As a result, it is the database requirements of engineering design activities in general that provide the motivation for object-oriented databases. In this book, however, we concentrate on software engineering merely as typifying those requirements.

1.6 SUMMARY

An understanding of the background to, and motivation for, applying database technology to computer-assisted design activities is an important precursor to any study in the object-oriented database area. In this chapter we have briefly examined this background with reference to the computer-assisted development of software. In particular, we have shown that controlling the managerial and administrative aspects of a large software project can be at least as important as the technical problems being addressed. Organizing teams of developers over an extended period of time requires positive support: this is one of the motivating factors in providing an integrated project support environment (IPSE).

At the heart of such an IPSE is some form of data storage facility. The basic characteristics of a database system—storage for large amounts of data, control of concurrent data access, services for recovery, and control of data integrity—appear ideally suited to software development data control. However, closer inspection has revealed a number of important properties of software development applications which can lead to problems with the use of traditional database architectures and mechanisms. This has fuelled interest in new approaches to database system development geared to computer-aided design applications, with the object-oriented approach to database systems being at the fore.

Thus, we have established two important points in this chapter:

- Support for software development should be centred on a database component.
- Traditional database systems prove largely unsuitable for use as the data management component of an IPSE.

2

OBJECT-ORIENTATION

If I hear the phrase 'everything is an object' once more, I think I will scream. (Stonebraker, 1988)

In the last few years there has been a increasing use of the term *object-oriented* in many areas of computer science. Programming languages, design methodologies, user interfaces, databases, and operating systems have all been described as object-oriented. While it is exciting to see a common theme linking these disparate areas, it soon becomes evident that the same term is being used in different ways in each of the different application areas. Indeed, a group of leading researchers from one of these domains found that there was little common understanding of the term even between themselves (Laguna Beach Participants, 1989).

Clearly then, it would be futile to attempt to provide here a single definition of what it means to be object-oriented. Rather, in this chapter we attempt to do two things. First, we describe a number of characteristics which appear to be common to systems, languages, and applications which describe themselves as object-oriented. Secondly, we examine something of the history and background of this term within computer science.

2.1 THE OBJECT-ORIENTED MODEL

The cornerstone of the object-oriented approach is that it provides a more natural way to model many real-world situations. The important point here is that the model obtained by using an object-oriented approach will be a more direct representation of the situation, providing a better framework for understanding and manipulating the complex relationships which may exist.

18

While implementations of object-oriented systems vary greatly, in whichever application area an object-oriented model is applied, a number of key characteristics can be identified. These are:

- support for object instances and classes;
- encapsulation of operations with data;
- specialization of objects.

2.1.1 Objects

In the object-oriented model the entities of interest are called *objects*. We cannot give a precise definition of what an object is. Rather, we can note a number of characteristics that objects possess. Depending on the application area, examples of objects may range from a complex chip design for a new CPU in a VLSI design system, right down to the single digit '7'. What these objects have in common is that each is uniquely identifiable, may have a number of data properties associated with it which record the current state of the object, and can be manipulated (i.e. can either have information about its state revealed, or have its state amended) through a well-defined set of operators. For example, each VLSI chip design will be uniquely identifiable, may have properties associated with it which record the date the design was last changed and who changed it, as well as recording the design itself, and can be manipulated with a fixed set of editing commands and tools which extend the design, verify its correctness, and so on.

The point about object identity is an important one. Many systems distinguish between different entities by examining the properties that they possess. Two entities are deemed to be the same if the current values of their properties are the same. This means that there is no way to distinguish between two different entities which happen at some point in time to have the same property values. In relational database systems for example, this problem arises and is overcome by associating a special property (or set of properties) called the *primary key* with each relational tuple. For any one relation, no two tuples of that relation are allowed to be assigned the same value simultaneously for the primary key. While this approach is satisfactory in some situations (e.g. a vehicle entity can be given a unique registration number property), there are others where an artificially contrived property must be invented purely for means of identification (e.g. a program module entity can be given a unique module number, distinct from all other module numbers in the system). Creating and maintaining these unique identifiers can require unnecessary work on behalf of the end user, as well as having a detrimental effect on the clarity and semantics capture of the real-world model being developed.

In object-oriented systems a distinction is made between an object's identity and its properties. When an object is created a unique, system-generated identifier is associated with that object for its entire lifetime. This provides a unique handle on the object, allowing the system to differentiate between the two different kinds of comparison that can be made:

1. Identity. *Is object A the same object as object B?*
   Answered by comparing the identifiers of A and B.

2. Equality. *Does object A have the same value as object B?*
   Answered by comparing the properties of A and B.

Finally, as a way of organizing objects in a more manageable way, objects which have the same kinds of properties, and can be manipulated using similar operators, are classified to form distinct object *classes*.[1] For example, the digits '7' and '8' respond to the same operators (addition, subtraction, and so on) and can be said to be instances of a single class we may call `integer`. Hence, every object will be an instance, or representative, of some object class. The definition of the object class can act as a template for creating instances of the class. Each instance of a class has a unique identity, but has the same set of data properties (or state variables) and responds to the same set of operators (or methods).

2.1.2 Encapsulation

Implicit in the above description is the idea that we can define two distinct views of an object: one by focusing on its data properties, the other by focusing on its functional properties. In many systems (languages, methods, and so on) there is a strong built-in bias towards one or other of these views. For example, in database modelling the entity–relationship approach is strongly biased towards the data aspects of the real world, while the Jackson Structured Design (JSD) approach to systems analysis takes a strongly functional view of a system. Some systems, for example programming languages such as FORTRAN, Pascal and C, include facilities for modelling both the data and functional aspects of an application. However, these two views are for the most part kept separate. In many situations it is the integration of these two views which provides a more complete understanding of an application, and allows a more realistic model of the application to be created.

Hence, central to the object-oriented model is the concept that the entities of interest in the real world can be modelled most effectively by representing each real-world entity as an object in the model. The definition of such an object in-

---

[1] We have to be careful here about the terms *class* and *type*. They clearly are strongly related, but are used interchangeably by some people, and very differently by others. The most common interpretation treats *type* as an intensional definition of the characteristics of a set of objects, while *class* has an extensional meaning, denoting the set of objects which conform to the type at a given time. For this discussion we shall do no more than note that a number of different interpretations exist! See Beech (1988) for more details.

cludes both the data properties of that object and the operators which are permitted to manipulate that object. In this way, it is claimed that a move is made from representing the purely structural aspects of an object, or the purely functional aspects of an object, towards a more integrated behavioural view combining both state and operations which reveal or amend that state (Maier *et al.*, 1986). This is more closely tuned with the way in which we think about entities in the real world; we rarely divorce the concept of what the entity is (i.e. its state) from what we can do with it (i.e. operators which manipulate it).

For example, we can record information about programmers and their assignment to projects in a more natural way, if we encapsulate the data structures modelling this situation with the operations that effect those structures. An assignment object can represent the fact that a particular programmer has been assigned to a project, with the state recording the name of the programmer, the project name, the date the assignment was made, and so on. The operators 'make assignment' and 'delete assignment' may be defined to manipulate assignment objects. It is important to recognize that the definition of an assignment object tells you not only what it is, but also what you are allowed to do with it.

Thus, the essence of encapsulation is that such operators form an interface to assignment objects which provide the *only* way to amend the state of assignment objects. Hence, the user of an object has no way to access that object other than through the defined set of operators. This is very like a 'black box' approach to system description, where one (server) object provides a fixed set of services to another (client) object. The client object cannot attempt to manipulate or amend the server object other than through the set of services the server provides.

2.1.3 Specialization

We have already introduced the concept of object classification as a means of factoring out the definitions of common properties and operators on objects. The process can be carried one step further by recognizing that there are properties and operators which are common to object classes themselves. For example, if we have instances of an employee class and instances of a software engineer class, we will probably find that both classes of object have properties in common such as name, date of birth, and salary. They will also have similar operators for manipulation such as 'hire' and 'fire'. In fact, we will probably find that an instance of software engineer has all of the characteristics of an employee plus some more of its own. Using database terminology, we can describe software engineer as a specialization of the more general class of employee.[1] In general, we find that a subclass hierarchy can be defined in which a subclass is a specialization of its

---

[1]Conversely, we can also think of employee as a generalization of software engineer.

superclass in the hierarchy. Some system-defined root class is usually provided to start the whole thing off. For example, `software engineer` may be a subclass of `employee` which itself is a subclass of the system-defined root class `object`.

An important aspect of this specialization process is that we do not need to define each subclass from scratch. We can think of a new class as an existing class amended to fit our new requirements. In particular, we can think of a subclass as *inheriting* the behaviour of its superclass. In fact, we can be more general than that and imagine four different ways in which we can derive the behaviour of a subclass from the behaviour of its superclass:[1]

1. The subclass may inherit some or all of the behaviour of its superclass. For example, we could define the class `read-only files` as a specialization of the class `files` where `read-only files` has inherited the data properties of `files`, but only a subset of its operators (i.e. not the 'write' operator).

2. The subclass may inherit all of the behaviour of its superclass, and additionally define behaviour of its own. In the earlier example, we could envisage `software engineer` as inheriting all of the behaviour of `employee` and additionally defining new data properties (e.g. favourite programming language), and new operators (e.g. to assign a software engineer to fix a particular piece of code) specific to software engineers.

3. While the subclass may inherit the behaviour of its superclass, some of that behaviour may be redefined, or overridden. For example, in an object-oriented windowing system, a `text document` class may redefine the operator 'display' which it has inherited from its parent class `screen object` to be more specific to the kind of object it represents. Hence, although the same operator name is used, the action that takes place is specific to the particular class of object to which the operator is applied.

4. Not only can a subclass override the behaviour of its superclass, but it may also access that overridden behaviour. Consider the `software engineer` example above. If the `software engineer` class inherits a 'hire' operator from the `employee` class, we may wish the 'hire' operator to do everything it did previously, but additionally to enroll the new software engineer on to the next available programming course. We can think of the new 'hire' operator as a call to the overridden 'hire' operator with some additional functionality.

So far we have assumed that a new class has a single immediate superclass in the class hierarchy. In some object-oriented systems this process is generalized even further to allow a subclass to be defined with several immediate superclasses. This is known as *multiple inheritance*. For example, if we also have a

---

[1] An actual implementation of an object-oriented system will permit some combination of these four approaches.

class consultant as a subclass of employee, then some objects may simultaneously be instances of software engineer and consultant. This new class of consultant software engineers is an immediate subtype of both software engineer and consultant and may inherit behaviour from both of its parent classes. The subclass graph for this example is illustrated in Fig. 2.1.

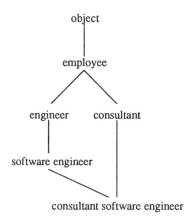

Figure 2.1   An example subclass graph

However, multiple inheritance is not without its problems. Illustrative of the issues which must be addressed in supporting a multiple inheritance scheme are the conflicts that arise when behaviour is inherited from two or more superclasses. For example, if both the software engineer and the consultant classes have independently defined an operator with the same name, what does this operator mean in the class consultant software engineer ?

To summarize, we note that one of the key characteristics of an object-oriented system is the flexibility that is provided by allowing new object classes to be defined, which gradually extend the class hierarchy through the process of specialization. In this way, the different kinds of objects of interest can gradually and incrementally be extended as our understanding of the application domain grows.

2.1.4   Advantages of the object-oriented model

Having briefly discussed the basic characteristics of object-oriented systems, we can identify a number of general advantages that are commonly claimed for the object-oriented approach. These are particular manifestations of the general principle of support for *abstraction*. That is, the ability to devise a model of a problem in terms of the data items and operators which are most suited to our needs. The internal details of the data and operators are ignored so that all we need to know is *what* they do, not *how* they do it. We can leave such details until later.

In addition, by allowing one object to be defined in terms of previously defined objects, the objects are defined and manipulated at increasing levels of abstraction at each level in the specialization hierarchy. The solution to a problem can then be defined at the most appropriate level of abstraction, using the objects defined at that level. This helps to reduce the complexity of applications, which is often increased by attempting to define a solution at an inappropriate level of abstraction.

Specific advantages which arise from direct support for abstraction include:

- *Data hiding.*   The internal state of an object is hidden from its users. As a result, the clients of an object need only concern themselves with the services the object provides, not the way in which those services are provided. For example, suppose we wish to make use of a set of graphical operations for a windowing system. If there is an operator to bring a window to the foreground, we only need to know how to call it, not how it implements its internal algorithms. Thus, not only are clients of an object not distracted by the irrelevant internal mechanisms used to implement the object's behaviour, they are also unable to access the private parts of the server object's state.

- *Data independence.* By restricting the use of an object to a fixed set of operators, we are able to control the extent to which the client object relies on the internal details of the server object. In particular, if the internal algorithms of the server object are amended, we are able to insulate the client from those changes provided the interface to the server object remains unchanged (i.e. the same operators still exist).

- *Modularity.* The definition of appropriate objects can act as the focal point for modularizing the implementation of a large software system, often providing a boundary for distribution or concurrency of objects. The object-oriented approach naturally encourages designs involving a small number of relatively independent object types interacting in well-defined ways.

- *Reuse.* By organizing the classes within a specialization hierarchy, common properties of a class can be filtered out and inherited by subclasses. In this way common state variables and methods need not be reimplemented, but can be shared between classes. This is an example of component reuse, providing many benefits to the system implementor and maintainer. In addition, by identifying the main object classes within an application, the object-oriented approach lends itself to the creation of class libraries in which commonly used object classes are maintained. Then, not only are we encouraged to reuse objects within a single system through object specialization, but also reuse between different systems is facilitated through shared object libraries.

Many other advantages are claimed for the object-oriented model as it is applied in each of the different application areas. In the next section we examine those advantages, focusing on object-orientation as it has been applied within particular application domains.

2.2   THE ORIGINS OF THE OBJECT-ORIENTED MODEL

While interest in the object-oriented approach can be found in many application areas, it is clear that many different reasons are being given for making use of this approach. It may be useful at this point to review the original difficulties found in these areas, and show how the object-oriented model has been used to provide a general framework for their solution. Rather than attempt to examine exhaustively each application domain, we instead look briefly at two of the fields which have most strongly embraced object-oriented concepts and techniques: programming languages and software engineering. These descriptions act as a precursor to later sections in which we examine in more detail how the database systems field is also adopting an object-oriented approach.

2.2.1   Programming languages

Human beings come to understand the world and solve the problems with which they are faced by means of a process we call *abstraction*. For example, when trying to understand how a car works in order to be able to fix it, we need to know something about engines, gears and the things we can do to them. However, when learning to drive a car, we abstract from our knowledge of how the car works and concentrate on manipulating the steering wheel, depressing the accelerator, and so on (Booch, 1987). These are different ways of viewing the same objects, with emphasis being placed on different functional roles.

Similarly, since programs are written to deal with real-world problems, the more closely the data structures and operations they use mirror those embodied in the problem being tackled, the more likely they are to be correct, extendible and maintainable. To facilitate this, various mechanisms for abstraction have been built into programming languages (Shaw, 1984; Bishop, 1986).

Most modern programming languages provide facilities to combine the primitives of the language into higher level or more abstract operations which we call *procedures*. In addition, by making it possible to call procedures from within procedures, a way of extending the primitives of the language is provided which allows them to be used in an increasingly abstract way. Procedural abstraction provides an elegant means of modularizing and successively decomposing a program into components and therefore reducing the programming tasks to easily understood and manageable tasks.

Similarly, programming languages have primitive *data types* such as 'integer', 'character', and so on. A data type is normally considered to comprise not only the data structure itself but also the operations which manipulate it. For example, the data type 'integer' in Pascal incorporates not only the structure for containing all integers in the range of the machine being used, but also the operations add, subtract, and so on for combining instances of this type. In fact no other operations can be used to manipulate instances of the data type except those specified by its type definition.

However, programmers seldom wish to work with such low-level types. For example, a problem may require the use of complex numbers, in which case it would obviously be helpful if the language offered such a type together with the operations with which to manipulate instances of the complex number type. Since it is not possible to provide primitive data types covering all the possible types which programmers might require, modern programming languages such as Modula and Ada provide mechanisms for defining new data types (called *abstract data types* or *ADTs*), with their own special operations to manipulate them. Some important points concerning ADTs are as follows:

- Provided new ADTs can be defined in terms of existing ADTs as well as primitive data types, this mechanism provides a very powerful means of extending the data types we can work with.

- Procedural abstraction is vital to the ADT mechanism, since it gives the power to create the new operations which manipulate the new data type.

- Inherent in the ADT mechanism is the concept of enforcing the new type. Only the operations defined within an ADT can be used to manipulate the type. In Pascal, for example, it is possible to simulate the creation of a new data type (e.g. using a linked list to simulate a first-in–last-out queue). However, it is not possible to enforce the type since there is nothing to stop the queue being accessed as though it were a linked list.

- The ADT mechanism also provides an appropriate degree of 'information hiding' in the sense that if we have defined a queue ADT, the users of that ADT can only see the data structure as a queue. They know nothing about how it is implemented (e.g. whether as an array, or a linked list, or whatever). This allows the writer of an ADT and its users to be independent, with a controlled interface between them for communication. This in turn greatly facilitates decomposition of a program into separate tasks, which may be carried out independently by different people.

While the first high-level programming languages experimented with some of the ideas of ADTs, the main landmark in this work was the language Simula

(Dahl and Nygaard, 1966). This language was intended primarily for writing simulation programs. Its designers recognized the requirement in such applications for introducing higher level concepts for modelling real-world objects. The main addition to the language allowed both data and operators to be defined in a single syntactic unit called a *class*.

Two of the most influential systems to build on the ideas of Simula were:

- *Actor languages.* These languages use the concept of active 'actors' within a system which carry out tasks in response to the messages sent to them (Agha, 1986). An actor consists of a data part and a procedural part, organized into a hierarchy with inheritance of data and operators from parent to child actors in the hierarchy.

- *Smalltalk.* Originally designed for a new design of hardware at the Xerox Palo Alto Research Centre, Smalltalk is a complete programming language and development environment based on object-oriented principles (Goldberg and Robson, 1983). The underlying concept, that the real world is modelled as a set of objects communicating via message passing, has formed the basis of a great deal of subsequent object-oriented development. In many ways, Smalltalk has been one of the major catalysts in generating interest in object-oriented systems.

More recently the power and flexibility of programming languages has been extended even further by applying the notion of abstraction support more generally and uniformly within the programming language. Languages such as Objective-C, C++, and Eiffel are based on the philosophy of support for ADTs. Rather than refer to an ADT with some procedures which can be called with suitable parameters, the terminology used is that of *objects* which respond to *messages* to invoke *methods* on object instances. By introducing object classification, these languages allow a more powerful organizational structure to be imposed on the objects. Inheritance of behaviour between object classes further enhances the modularity and data hiding within a program, and also provides a measure of reuse of methods between objects.

2.2.2 Software engineering

Many of the arguments used above for programming languages apply equally well to other phases in the software development life-cycle. In particular, we can think of software development as the process of creating a series of models of the real world at different levels of abstraction, and with varying levels of completeness, in order to capture the many distinct kinds of information which must be processed. Figure 2.2 depicts the software development life-cycle for a software project.

At each phase of the project a representation, or model, of the application system is developed using some language or notation. One representation is produced via

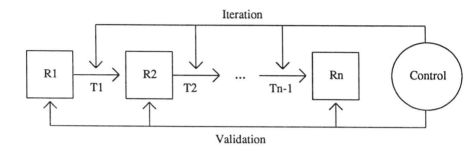

Figure 2.2   A general life-cycle model for a software project

some transformation from a previous representation. In Fig. 2.2 these representations are labelled R1 to Rn, and the transformations are labelled T1 to Tn-1.

The basis of software development is to verify that each of these models is internally correct with respect to the portion of the real world under consideration, and to validate that each of the models is correct with respect to the others (i.e. no information becomes corrupt or lost during transformation from one representation to another). This leads to each representation being iteratively developed. In Fig. 2.2 the control component is responsible for initiating and monitoring the validation and iteration feedbacks which are necessary between the representations that are produced.

The arguments presented in the previous section encourage an object-oriented approach to be applied to the coding phase of a software project. The model of the real world which corresponds to the coding phase will be developed using the object-oriented programming language chosen.

However, we can equally well extend the arguments to other phases in the project life-cycle. In particular, in the systems specification and design phases that precede the coding phase, most existing modelling formalisms have been developed to provide languages in which to represent the design aspects of a system. These languages vary widely, from structured modelling techniques such as JSD (Sutcliffe, 1988) and SSADM (Downs et al., 1988), to more formal specification languages such as Z (Woodcock and Loomes, 1988) and VDM (Jones, 1986). What is apparent from many of these techniques is that they force a representation of the real-world system which is biased towards either a data-oriented view, or a process-oriented view of the world. Typically, the choice of modelling formalism is made on the basis of whether the application can be considered primarily as data-centred or process-centred.

This has given rise to the promotion of an object-oriented view of system design in which a balance is provided between data and process modelling. The principles of the approach match closely those of object-oriented programming languages, as described above. However, the approach provides a number of advantages for the design phases. In particular, the use of an object as a unit of modularity also provides a convenient unit of sharing between groups of designers, allowing large system specifications and designs to be divided among a group of software engineers along object boundaries. Each object provides a unit of consistency, concurrency, and distribution within the project.

Hence, the past few years have seen increasing interest in object-orientation as it applies to each of the life-cycle phases. For example:

- Object-oriented requirements analysis (OORA) techniques have been developed which involve early identification of candidate objects and their interrelationships. The objects are organized into classes, have both state and operational aspects, and so on. The requirements definition consists of documentation describing these objects, together with (graphical) descriptions of their possible interrelationships (Coad and Yourdon, 1990).

- Object-oriented specification languages are an attempt to try to impose an object-oriented framework on to existing specification languages. For example, the object-oriented approach may be particularly useful as a structuring framework for developing and browsing large specifications in a language such as Z (Dahl, 1987).

- Object-oriented design (OOD) techniques have been under investigation for a number of years. As an extension of the OORA techniques described above, in object-oriented design methods such as HOOD (CISI-Ingenierie/MATRA, 1986) or Booch's method (Booch, 1982), the notion of an object is used as the primary focus for structuring information.

Clearly, it is not essential to use an object-oriented approach in all of the phases of software development. For example, an object-oriented system design need not necessarily be implemented in an object-oriented programming language. However, by doing so a cleaner conceptual mapping between the design and coding phases of a project is provided. Indeed, as it is the management of the relationships between the many system models that is a major factor in the success or failure of a large software project, particularly in the event of errors, omissions, and enhancements to those models, a unified view of the full software life-cycle is particularly important.

2.3 SUMMARY

In many cases, the rapid and widespread adoption of the object-oriented approach has resulted in the underlying principles of the approach being buried under an avalanche of implementation details and specific mechanisms, leading to misconceptions and much confusion. There is clearly an important requirement to extract the main concepts of the object-oriented approach, and to present them in as clear and simple a way as possible, before attempting to show how those concepts apply to a particular application area.

This chapter has concentrated on three basic principles of the object-oriented approach: objects and object classes, encapsulation of operators with objects, and organization of object classes into a hierarchy through object specialization. These have been presented as the main underlying concepts of the object-oriented approach as it has been applied to the different application areas.

The next chapter will expand on these principles with particular emphasis on the way in which they have been applied to the database field.

OBJECT-ORIENTED DATABASES

Much of the recent work in database research has been concentrated on *object-oriented database systems*. While the excitement has been likened to a 'religious fervour' (King, 1989), it is becoming clear that a wide interpretation of the term exists, leading to much confusion (Laguna Beach Participants, 1989). In this chapter we clarify the present situation in two ways. Firstly, the many and varied influences on object-oriented database work are described. This provides the background required for understanding why such a diversity of systems and applications are moving towards object-orientation. Secondly, we extract some of the main characteristics of present-day object-oriented databases.

The chapter concludes with an examination of a number of important issues which are currently the focus of much attention by object-oriented database researchers. These give an introduction to the problems, approaches, and open issues which are currently being addressed.

3.1 WHY OBJECT-ORIENTATION IN DATABASES?

The application of database technology to data processing systems brought a number of notable improvements. In particular, security and integrity of recorded data were enhanced by reducing redundantly stored data, and end-user application programs became easier to write and maintain owing to the data independence that database systems provided (Date, 1986). Recognizing these improvements, it was a natural step to try to widen the application of database systems from the data processing realm to other areas. Statistical databases and bibliographic databases are two fields which are benefiting from this approach.

However, although database techniques are quite mature, it soon becomes clear that their direct application to new areas may not produce the same measure of improvements. This is mainly due to differences in the characteristics of the different application domains. Not only does the data to be stored have different characteristics, but there are also noticeable differences in the kinds of relationships between data, user access patterns to the data, and the variety of users who wish to access the data. One field in which this is particularly apparent is in the development of environments to support activities such as VLSI design, architectural design, and software design. As we noted in Chapter 1, design data is often complex and variable in length, may be highly interrelated, and may evolve rapidly over time, though old versions of data items are often required to be maintained. This is in marked contrast to the fixed-length, slowly evolving data which characterizes data processing applications.

While the work on applying database technology to design applications is acting as a catalyst for much of the present database research, there are a number of important continuing research trends which are of direct significance in the move towards object-orientation in database systems.

3.1.1   Complete system = application programs + database

In defining a database schema a user is producing a model of some real-world system. The aim is to produce a representation whose state at any instant in time closely resembles the state of the real world. Hence, the database must provide mechanisms for ensuring that a fairly direct representation of the real world can be produced. This implies that facilities must be provided to model the different kinds of entity which are found in the real world, and the varied and complex relationships which exist between those entities. In addition, the operations which reveal or amend the state must be constrained to ensure that the model does not become out of step with respect to the real world.

While the data model supported by a database system allows information about many aspects of the real world to be captured and controlled, there is usually a great deal of information which cannot be directly represented. Hence, where a typical system consists of a set of application programs making use of the database services, some processing which is common to all applications may be duplicated in various application programs. As this processing is neither centrally controlled, nor consistently shared between all applications, it may lead to unnecessary duplication, omissions, and errors. A concern for many years has been to try to shift the balance within systems between user application programs and the database system to make the database responsible for as much of the processing as possible, as illustrated in Fig. 3.1.

The result will not only be a reduction in the burden to application programmers, but it should also produce more consistent systems which can be maintained and

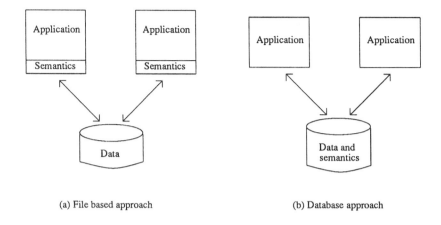

(a) File based approach   (b) Database approach

Figure 3.1   Application programs, data, and data semantics

may evolve with much less programming effort.

One aspect of this has been the work on semantic data modelling.

3.1.2   Capturing semantics in a database

Since Codd's original description of the relational data model (Codd, 1970) there
has been a growing level of acceptance of his ideas. Indeed at present, relational
developments account for a large majority of database research work, and many
relationally based database products are available. To a large degree, the main
reason for the application and use of the relational model in preference to others
has been the model's inherent conceptual simplicity: the basis of the model is the
single table-like structure known as a relation, manipulated by a closed algebra of
set-based operations.

However, it has been recognized that the elegance of such a simple conceptual
data model is limited to its use in modelling applications where the data is confined
to a small number of different types related in well-defined ways. Its use is limited
when it is applied to complex, highly structured application domains. In particular, the basic relational model cannot capture and control much of the semantics
of complex applications with such a simple framework. For example, although
the relational model enforces referential integrity,[1] it has no mechanism for distinguishing (and hence enforcing) the different kinds of relationship which may exist

---

[1] As one entity A is related to another entity B by recording the value of B's key field as an
attribute of A, referential integrity checks that the referenced entity B does currently exist in the
database. Attempts to delete B would fail while the relationship between A and B exists.

between entities. It would be useful, for example, to represent the relationship between a program and its documentation as an existence-dependent link: if the program is deleted, we would also delete the related documentation. However, if we also record the relationship between the program and the programmer who created the program, we would recognize that this relationship is not existence-dependent: deleting a program does not imply that the programmer must be deleted, or vice versa. A number of different kinds of relationship can be distinguished, including associations (many–many links), designations (one–many links), and characterizations (one–many existence-dependent links). If such distinctions are made, it is possible to define the semantics of operations to create, update, and delete instances of relationships differently for each case.

Recognizing some of the inadequacies of the relational model, new data models have been defined, often as extensions to the relational data model, which are more expressive, and which can capture more of the semantics of the application domain. Such models have come to be called *semantic data models*, though this term should probably be read as '*more* semantic data models' in comparison with the relational data model (Hull and King, 1987; Tsichritzis and Lochovsky, 1982; Brodie *et al.*, 1984).

As the main aim in semantic data models is to provide mechanisms for improving the representation of data, they usually include a rich set of structural abstractions which can be used by the data modeller (King, 1989). For example, when designing a data model representation of an application domain, the semantic data models may provide facilities for differentiating between different kinds of data entity, related through various kinds of relationship (e.g. entity A could be related to entity B through a sub/supertype relationship, via another associative entity, or even through an existence-dependent link).

When these different entities and relationships are distinguished, and made explicit in the data model, operators which manipulate those entities can take account of their associated semantics. For example, the operator 'delete entity' when applied to an entity representing a software project, may first have to find out if that project is involved in any assignment relationships with company employees, or has spawned any subprojects, before deciding on the actions implied by deleting that entity. In particular, the effect of the operation should not adversely affect the integrity of the database.

In this way, by distinguishing the many kinds of entity and relationship types that can exist, greater scope exists to be more expressive in representing the semantics of the application domain. However, a notable absence from these models is increased support for the manipulation of data. That is, the extended data structuring mechanisms are usually accompanied by the same general set of operators (i.e. 'create entity', 'delete entity', and 'update entity'). We are able to create and constrain the data structures more naturally if we recognize that the data structures that have been defined are accessed and updated through a fixed set of data type specific operators. For example, on creating a new entity it is often necessary to carry out a number of checks on other data entities before allowing the new entity to be created. Additionally, it may be necessary to invoke other operations as a consequence of this new entity being created. These checks and operations are entity-type specific. If we are creating a new employee entity, for example, we may check the existing data to see if this employee has previously been employed with the company, and once we have created the new employee entity, we may automatically assign this employee to the next available training course. Thus, the 'create entity' operator for the employee type will be different from the 'create entity' operator for, say, the project type.

Hence, the next stage in semantic data modelling is the integration of operator definition with the data structuring facilities such that operator definitions are entity-type specific. The object-oriented paradigm may be seen as one way to attempt this integration, providing a mechanism for progressing from a purely structural model of data towards a more *behavioural model*, combining facilities for both the representation and manipulation of data within the same model.

3.1.3   Making database systems computationally complete

Another interesting aspect of the interfacing of application programs with a database comes from a recognition that the processing power available in most existing database systems is severely limited.

The data manipulation language provided in a relational database system is said to be *relationally complete* if it can (at least) be shown to have expressive power equivalent to the relational algebra (or calculus) as defined by Codd (1970). However, to be more widely useful for developing applications, data manipulation languages also require additional features (Ullman, 1988). Typically, these include:

- arithmetic operations which allow the data values to be involved in arbitrary computations;

- print and display operations to allow relations and relation fragments to be displayed;

- aggregate functions (such as sum, count, and average) to be applied to columns of a relation.

Languages which allow any arbitrary arithmetic computation to be performed on data values can be referred to as *computationally complete*.

Databases which use SQL as the language for database access are a prime example of systems with a data manipulation language which is relationally complete, but not computationally complete. If you want to try to perform some simple manipulation of any data as either input to, or on results obtained from, an SQL query, there is no alternative but to embed the SQL statements within a conventional programming language. The programming language provides the manipulative capability which is missing from the database system alone, making the resulting combination computationally complete. Hence, to be more generally applicable, the database system must provide the mechanisms for embedding the database language within a conventional programming language (usually known as the *host language*).

While this solution is acceptable in many situations, and is widely used, there are a number of drawbacks. Most important of all is that programming languages and databases use different models of data and this makes the integration artificial and forced. Much of the application program is devoted to converting between the two models; for example, from program variables in the programming language's type system to fields of relational tuples in the database, and vice versa. Writing such applications is cumbersome, time-consuming, prone to error, and not standardized between different systems. A more seamless integration may reduce many of these problems (Moss, 1989).

3.1.4   Adding persistence to a programming language

We have emphasized the importance of data management from a database viewpoint, but there is another approach which is also being investigated—from the point of view of extending traditional programming languages with new data management facilities.

One of the problems with many of the programming languages which deal with data as complex, highly interrelated objects is that there are no facilities in the language to record these objects in a data store that persists between program invocations, other than at the granularity of a file (Atkinson and Buneman, 1987). As a result, much time and effort is spent within application programs converting from structured, object format to flat, unstructured file format, and vice versa. Attempts to address this problem have progressed in three ways:

1.   The addition of new constructs in existing programming languages to support a database model. For example, the addition of relational constructs into the programming language Pascal (Schmidt, 1977).

2.   The design of programming languages which can interact with data in a persistent store. For example, the languages PLAIN (Wasserman, 1979) and RIGEL (Rowe and Shoens, 1979) are specifically designed for the construction of database applications.

3.   The development of techniques which use the constructs already available in an existing programming language to support persistent data.

PS-Algol is an example of such an approach (Atkinson *et al.*, 1981; Atkinson and Buneman, 1987), with the PISA project (Atkinson *et al.*, 1987) continuing the work to investigate machine architectures capable of supporting a persistent language approach.

This last approach to persistent filestores is seen as a possible way to break the (often artificial) distinction between programming languages and databases.

This work has been recently taken up in the object-oriented programming community. Essentially, programs written in these languages spend much of their time building up complex object structures only to have to flatten this structure in order to save the objects in persistent store (e.g. to write them out to a file). To share objects between programs, the underlying file system mechanisms must be used for concurrency control, locking, security, and so on. These mechanisms tend not to be those required within many applications. As a result, interest is moving towards adding some sort of persistent object store to object-oriented programming languages (Copeland and Maier, 1984), and providing improved mechanisms for controlled sharing of such entities between groups of users.

3.2   CHARACTERISTICS OF OBJECT-ORIENTED DATABASES

The terms 'object', 'object-oriented' and 'object-orientation' are being used more and more frequently within the database community. While there appears to be little consensus on the meaning of these terms, it is possible to define a number of general characteristics exhibited by such systems. These appear mainly to concern support for the complex internal structure of the entities of interest in the perceived application domains, particularly their hierarchical nature and the complex network of relationships in which they are involved, coupled with other properties such as the importance of retaining unique object identifiers, and the usefulness of maintaining entities in a number of related versions.

In this section we examine these characteristics as they apply to database systems using a very broad definition of object-oriented databases which was introduced by Dittrich (1986). His informal definition of object-oriented database systems embraces any database system which is based on a data model that allows each real-world entity, regardless of its complexity, to be represented by a single data model object. Issues of object identity, abstraction, and operator encapsulation are then seen as manifestations of this basic principle. We examine these concepts below.

It is important to note, however, that although this definition of object-oriented databases concentrates on the data model aspects of the database, there are important considerations with regard to the other system services provided by a database system (e.g. recovery, security, transaction management, concurrency control).

These issues are addressed in later sections of this chapter.

3.2.1 Complex objects

In a number of applications we are interested in modelling objects which not only participate in relationships with other objects, but also have an internal structure consisting of smaller sub-objects involved in their own relationships. We can refer to objects with internal structure as *complex objects*.[1] There are many examples of applications in which complex objects can be found, but we will concentrate mainly on modelling of the software development process. In this domain, typical examples of complex objects are:

- *programs* consisting of modules, statements, declarations, and so on;
- *libraries* consisting of a number of programs and modules;
- *documents* consisting of a number of sections, subsections, and so on.

When modelling complex objects such as these, many systems ignore the internal structure of the objects completely and hide the internal structure of the object within an attribute of that object. For example, a program entity can have an attribute 'text' which holds the code associated with the program. The fine-grained information concerning subprograms and their interrelationships is buried within this attribute. Clearly, this approach severely restricts the semantics capture of the model. The main disadvantage of this approach is that commonplace queries regarding the internal structure of a complex object become difficult to satisfy, as this information is not explicitly recorded. Similarly, explicit control of the internal structure of the complex object cannot be enforced by the normal database mechanisms.

An alternative approach is to hold explicitly the internal structure of a complex object as entities and relationships in their own right. For example, we not only have a program entity, but also a number of subprogram entities which are related to the program entity through the relationship 'consists-of', say. We examine the problems of this approach with reference to a simple example.

Consider the use of a database to record information concerning source code and its interrelationships. Each program can be considered to have a name, an author, and other such attributes. A program is built from a number of program modules, which themselves have names, authors, and so on. Each module can itself be composed of other modules. Modules with a common theme can be collected together into a library. An example of such a situation is shown in Fig. 3.2, which is adapted from an example in Dittrich *et al.* (1987).

---

[1]Also used in the literature are the terms *molecular objects* (Batory and Buchmann, 1984) and *composite objects* (Kim *et al.*, 1987).

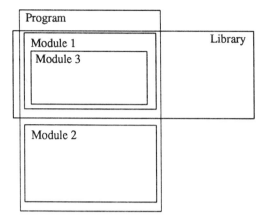

Figure 3.2   An example of programs, modules, and libraries

In Fig. 3.2 a program is shown to be composed of the modules Module 1 and Module 2. Module 1 includes Module 3. Also, Module 1 and Module 3 are drawn from a Library of modules. In this example we can consider 'Program', 'Module', and 'Library' as three examples of complex object types; all three have their own internal structure consisting of other entities. We can represent this example easily enough in a traditional database system. Fig. 3.3 shows an outline of an entity–relationship (E–R) schema which could be used to represent the example. However, while the relationships themselves can be captured, no distinction is made between the *external* relationships between different object types, and relationships which are *internal* to an object. The effect of this is that the model does not allow us to abstract the external relationships information easily while hiding the internal details. This not only makes the diagram (and hence its implementation) more difficult to follow, but also means that it is almost impossible to change the internal structure of any of the objects without making this visible to all users—even if the changes do not affect their use of the data.

Data models which allow complex objects to be represented directly have come to be called *structurally object-oriented* (Dittrich, 1986; King, 1989). For example, in the DAMOKLES system (Dittrich *et al.*, 1987), the example of Fig. 3.2 could be represented by the definition in Fig. 3.4.

By explicitly defining the complex structure of objects, users of an object can abstract from these details by ignoring the STRUCTURE IS clause of an object definition to obtain a higher level view of the object definition. The database system itself can take account of the structure in controlling the integrity of the application being represented.

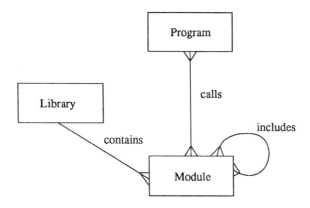

Figure 3.3   An E–R representation of programs, modules, and libraries

```
OBJECT TYPE program        OBJECT TYPE module         OBJECT TYPE library
   ATTRIBUTES                 ATTRIBUTES                 ATTRIBUTES
      name  : STRING[30]         name  : STRING[30]         name  : STRING[30]
      author: STRING[20]         author: ...                ...
   STRUCTURE IS module        STRUCTURE IS module        STRUCTURE IS module
END program                 END module                 END library
```

Figure 3.4   An example of an object definition in the DAMOKLES system

3.2.2   Object identity

A related issue in this context is object identity. While this concept is adequately covered in programming language systems, in database systems the entities represented are typically accessed by reference to particular attributes of an entity (e.g. the department entity whose name is Computer Science). However, there are numerous problems with only allowing objects to be identified via their properties. For example, what happens to an object when those attribute values change—is it still the same object? Similarly, maintaining consistency of relationships between objects is a significant overhead when the value of the attribute which identifies an object is amended.

To overcome these problems, the notion of object identity is distinguished from an object's current value. While the latter is allowed to change, the former is unique, system generated, never reused, and thus identifies a single object for its complete lifetime. The use of unique identifiers for database objects has been a feature of semantic data models for a number of years under the name of *surrogates* (Codd, 1979; Meier and Lorie, 1983).

3.2.3   User-defined operators

A further problem with the E–R representation of Fig. 3.3 concerns the manipulation of the objects represented. If we imagine that we have a relational implementation of Fig. 3.3, then any operation on the complex objects will require the user to bring together explicitly all of the component parts of that object before the operation can be performed. For example, to delete a library object, explicit delete commands must be issued to all of the modules in the library before the library entity itself can be deleted. This not only requires greater intellectual effort on behalf of the user, it also reduces the modularity and data hiding effects of the data model. As an illustration of this, imagine that we change the structure of a library to allow programs also to be stored in a library. The delete operation for a library is now different, and the user must modify the set of operations required to delete a library accordingly.

Hence, structural object-orientation is usually accompanied by mechanisms which allow operators to be defined over those complex objects. The operators are object class specific, in that a set of operators can be defined which are appropriate to a particular class of objects. For the library object class, for example, it may be appropriate to define operators which allow the current state of a library object to be revealed, or to make some changes to that state. Typical operators could include:

- 'last-update'—return the date of the most recent addition to a library;

- 'add-to-library'—insert a module into a library (and check it is not already there);

- 'is-in-library'—see if a module is in a library, and if so, return some information about that module.

It is important to note that if the structural definition of the library object changes, it is the responsibility of the database administrator to ensure that the operators will perform the correct actions (or are amended to do so). The user of those operators (e.g. in an application program) should be unaffected by the changes.

In addition to providing structural support for complex objects, database systems which provide this level of operational support can be called *operationally object-oriented* (Dittrich, 1986).

3.2.4   Encapsulation

Providing a set of generic database manipulation operators for complex objects increases the ease with which the database can be used. However, the low-level 'insert', 'update', and 'delete' operators are rarely the level at which we wish to manipulate complex objects. Rather, such operators are combined to perform more complex operators. For example, an operator to remove a module from a library would probably have to check that the module was not currently in use by any programs before removing it from the library. Of course, these higher level operators are specific to each complex object type.

Recognizing the need for a specific set of operators to be defined for each complex object type, a number of database systems allow the definer of a new object type not only to give the structure of that class of object, but also to define the set of operators with which the user can access and manipulate such objects. We can say that the operators are *encapsulated* with the structural definition of the object.

By ensuring that the defined operators for an object provide the only way to access that object, we provide an interface to the object which is user defined, specific to each class of object, and hides the implementation of the object from users of the object. Rather than a purely structural description of the object, we can say that a *behavioural* description has been given (i.e. structure plus operators). Database systems which provide this level of support can be said to be *behaviourally object-oriented* (Dittrich, 1986; King, 1989).

3.2.5   Class hierarchies and inheritance

So far the description of object-oriented databases has not explicitly referred to a number of concepts which appear to play a key role in object-oriented programming. In particular, we have not built our definition of object-oriented databases around a class hierarchy with inheritance between classes. The reason for this is to broaden the scope of database systems which come under the definition. While some object-oriented database systems are based around a class hierarchy with structural and behavioural inheritance between classes (the 'Smalltalk with persistent objects' approach), there are a number of other approaches which can also be classed as object-oriented. Adding programming language procedures to a relational database as in the POSTGRES system is one such approach (Stonebraker, 1986), while the non-first normal form data models such as N^2F^2 (Kuspert *et al.*, 1987) are another.

Hence, while useful in organizing classes into a meaningful framework, we can view class hierarchies and inheritance as optional features which are independent of the classification of object-oriented databases that we have presented.

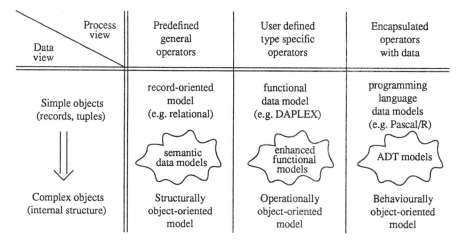

Process view / Data view	Predefined general operators	User defined type specific operators	Encapsulated operators with data
Simple objects (records, tuples) ⇓ Complex objects (internal structure)	record-oriented model (e.g. relational) *semantic data models* Structurally object-oriented model	functional data model (e.g. DAPLEX) *enhanced functional models* Operationally object-oriented model	programming language data models (e.g. Pascal/R) *ADT models* Behaviourally object-oriented model

Figure 3.5   A summary of the classification of object-oriented databases

3.2.6 Summary

We can summarize our classification of object-oriented databases using Fig. 3.5. This gives a data-oriented view of databases via the rows of the table, and a process-oriented view of database systems via the columns of the table. Object-oriented data models are concerned with complex data objects (i.e. objects that have an arbitrarily complex internal structure). The attitude that they exhibit towards operators classifies the object-oriented database as either structural, operational, or behavioural.

It is important to note that the table is in fact a discrete representation of what is a continuous spectrum along both the data and process axes. Hence, in the first column, 'Predefined general operators', the boundary between record-oriented and structurally object-oriented models is straddled by a host of what are usually called 'semantic data models', or 'extended relational models'. For example, models such as RM/T (Codd, 1979), the entity–relationship model (E–R) (Chen, 1976) and E–ER (Elmasri and Navathe, 1989) provide a number of data structuring mechanisms which bring them closer to structurally object-oriented data models. Similarly, the bridge between functional data models and operationally object-oriented data models is provided by enhanced functional models such as TAXIS (Mylopoulos and Wong, 1980). These models concentrate on the process aspects of the data model, often at the expense of the data structuring primitives. Finally, the models which attempt to encapsulate operators with data type definitions include extensions to programming languages such as Pascal/R (Schmidt, 1977). A different approach, moving towards the behaviourally object-oriented systems, is to allow attributes of a relation to be defined as operators in the database query language. For example, in POSTGRES (Stonebraker, 1986) the QUEL language can be used as the domain of a relational attribute.

3.3   ISSUES

While the previous section identifies the main characteristics of the data models supported by object-oriented database systems, there are a wide range of further issues which must be addressed. In the main these issues arise either as a direct consequence of the characteristics that have been identified, or must be faced in attempting to embody those characteristics within a particular system. We shall now examine a number of those issues under the broad headings of *data model aspects*, *system functions*, and *implementation considerations*.

3.3.1   Data model aspects

Query language

A vital component of any database system is the *query language* which provides the interface between user and database system. In most database systems a number of different languages may be provided for accessing data at different abstract levels (e.g. physical storage level, conceptual level, or end-user level). At the higher levels, the database system must provide facilities for specifying queries in an *ad hoc* manner, at the discretion of the database end user. In addition, the query language must be (Atkinson *et al.*, 1989):

- declarative, allowing relatively complex data structures to be interrogated using a simple query;

- efficient, providing obvious handles for query optimization;

- application-independent, enabling it to be used on a wide variety of database applications.

While the objectives of a query language are commonly accepted, in the case of object-oriented database systems a wide range of approaches have been taken in an attempt to achieve those objectives. We can classify the approaches into three broad categories.

First, some systems have used languages based on logic (e.g. G-Logis, the data language of G-Base (Graphael Inc., 1988), O_2 (Bancilhon, 1988), and TEDM (Zhu and Maier, 1988)). In TEDM, for example, queries resemble PROLOG clauses, with an *action* being performed if a *pattern* is matched against the database.

Second, in some object-oriented systems an existing relational database query language is extended with new functionality. This approach has most often been seen in the context of extending the SQL language with 'object-oriented' properties. In the Iris system, for example, the Object-SQL (OSQL) query language adds the concepts of object identity and multivalued properties (as described later in this section) to SQL, and also replaces the notion of a relation by types and (user-defined) functions (Beech, 1988). These functions can be used in the 'where' and 'select' clauses of a query.

Third, some systems extend a programming language with appropriate persistent data structuring facilities. As programming languages already include facilities for data definition and manipulation (data definition through the language's type system, and data manipulation using predefined arithmetic functions within procedures and subroutines), for an object-oriented database query language the main requirement is to extend these mechanisms to allow data types which persist across program executions. Different approaches to persistent programming languages are being investigated. Examples of one such approach are OPAL, the query language of the GemStone system (Ullman, 1988), which extends the Smalltalk programming language with a declarative notation for set expressions, and the query language of ONTOS, which is based on the C++ programming language extended with a persistent object store for C++ classes (Ontologic Inc., 1989).

The main debate between the different possible approaches to the design of object-oriented database query languages centres on the 'seamlessness' (or otherwise) of the integration between the data definition and manipulation languages of the query language, and the application programming language (Joseph *et al.*, 1989). Embedding a database query language into a conventional programming language has long been the source of problems. An *impedance mismatch* often occurs between the different models of data embodied in both the query language and programming language (Atkinson, 1978). This is a source of confusion to application programmers, and can result in many inefficiencies in practice. Thus, the argument most often cited by proponents of the extended programming language approach is that their approach avoids the mismatch by enforcing a single data model—that of the (extended) programming language.

To counter this argument, those in favour of an extended relational query language point out that a 'seamless' approach precludes the possibility of a single 'standard' object-oriented database query language; in general, the typing systems of different programming languages are incompatible. Rather, they cite the advantages of a single, universal object-oriented database query language in a similar way to the use of SQL for relational systems. While SQL itself has a number of known limitations and inconsistencies, there is no doubt that there are many advantages from having a commonly understood relational query language. Indeed, if the 'standard' object-oriented database query language could be defined as some form of (upwardly compatible) extension of SQL, then further advantages of controlled system evolution, and compatibility with existing (relational) applications might also accrue. This would smooth the introduction of object-oriented database systems into industry (Beech, 1988).

Navigation vs. set operations

An interesting issue within an object-oriented database query language concerns the way in which end-user access to data takes place. It has been claimed that for many of the application domains in which object-oriented databases are applied, navigation from one object to another is by far the most common mode of data access (Bernstein, 1987). This is in contrast to the set-based operations which are the cornerstone of relational database systems. Hence, they claim that a query language based on navigation within the database schema is a better approach than attempting to define an algebra of operations over objects. Illustrative of this argument are examples such as browsing a parts explosion in a hardware design application, and exploring a hierarchy of documents in an office information system.

However, the limitations of navigational query languages have already been well documented in comparison with the relational model (Brown, 1989). The power of a set-based manipulated language, especially its associative nature within a closed algebra, is a major factor in providing a measure of data independence between applications and changes in data structures.

The debate is further complicated due to the fact that object-oriented database query languages allow user-defined operators to be part of a query. This can make the usual approaches to query optimization as used in relational (set-based) database languages much less efficient, particularly in a system which allows the user-defined functions to be expressed in a conventional programming language.

Computational completeness

One of the main reasons for the 'impedance mismatch' described earlier is that query languages for relational database systems are not computationally complete. As a result, in order to write an application program, the query language must be embedded in a host language which provides the additional computational primitives. Object-oriented database systems attempt to overcome this by providing a query language which *is* computationally complete, either by devising a completely new language (as in VBase (Andrews and Harris, 1987)) or by extending existing programming or database languages (as in OPAL (Ullman, 1988)). The result is that most[1] of the application is written in a single, consistent language, reducing

---

[1] As has been noted (Atkinson *et al.*, 1989), it may not be possible to write a complete application in this language as the language may be computationally complete, but not *resource* complete (e.g. no screen handling primitives).

confusion and eliminating many of the inefficiencies which occur in translating from one language to another.

Versions

The representation of multiple object versions is essential to many of the applications for object-oriented databases, in particular, engineering design activities. For example, versions of a VLSI circuit design, a computer program, and a requirement analysis document are all typical. As a result, most object-oriented database systems address the issue of representing, controlling and accessing object versions.

Three possible approaches can be distinguished.

1. Versions are so fundamental that the object-oriented data model includes primitives to deal with them as a central component of the model. The DAMOK-LES system (Dittrich *et al.*, 1987), and the Iris system (Fishman, 1989) are examples of this approach. In both of these systems types (or classes) can be defined as 'versionable'. As a result, instances of the type may have many versions identified by a version number. Primitive operators in the language can reference object versions, create new object versions, and so on.

2. Versions are not considered to be part of the data model itself, but instead a version service is provided by a layer of software implemented directly on top of the kernel data model. This approach has been adopted by the Encore system (Skarra *et al.*, 1986) which implements versioning and complex object services as a separate layer on top of its basic data model.

3. Versions are considered to be an application issue. Hence, rather than provide some model of version control in the database, the applications must set up their own types for recording version control, suited to their own particular needs. The GemStone system takes this approach (Maier and Stein, 1987), allowing version control information to be recorded by defining appropriate classes in the GemStone class hierarchy. By creating a version class, for example, its behaviour can be inherited by any of its user-defined subclasses. This could include properties such as 'version-number' and 'last-changed-date', and methods such as 'checkout-version'.

While each of the above techniques has good and bad points, there are notable advantages in applying the first of these approaches, integrating version services within the kernel data model. In particular, the version services can be used as the basis of other database mechanisms, namely for schema evolution and in concurrency control. Both of these are now discussed in more detail.

Schema evolution

Database systems are designed to control the recording of information which changes over time. However, implicit in traditional database systems is the fact that it is the data instances which will change, while the definition of the structure of the data (the database schema) will remain relatively static. Problems may arise when the schema is frequently changed. In particular, what happens to existing data instances which conform to the previous schema?

Unfortunately, schema evolution is much more of an issue in object-oriented database systems. The main reasons for this are a consequence of the application areas which are typically addressed by object-oriented databases. In particular, the applications tend to be:

- Exploratory in nature. As a result, it is expected that errors, omissions, and inconsistencies in the schema will be found throughout a project. Continual schema evolution is the result.

- Continually re-interpreted. It is the nature of design activities that during the life of a project new insights into the problem are gained. This often leads to additions and modifications of existing data definitions.

- Long-lived. There is a case for arguing that the large scale, complex applications which object-oriented databases are designed to address must be expected to be in use over many years. The large amount of resources which would be required to develop such applications often dictate that this is the case. Hence, the schema is likely to undergo many changes during its lifetime.

Two approaches to schema evolution can be found.

In the first approach, a set of rules is defined which describe the actions to be taken when the schema is modified in order to make existing data compatible with the new schema definition. For example, in the ORION database system a taxonomy of possible modifications to a database schema has been devised. For each possible type of change a set of rules for enforcing the correct semantics of that change have been defined (Kim *et al.*, 1989). This has been achieved by defining a set of invariants for any ORION database schema, and making sure that schema changes do not invalidate those invariants. Where a number of possible interpretations of a schema change exist, a set of conflict resolution rules have been defined.

The second approach is to extend the notion of versioning from the data instances to the data definitions themselves. Hence, a change to a type definition will produce a new version of that type definition. Any data instances will conform to one or more versions of a type definition. For example, one proposal by Zdonik (Skarra and Zdonik, 1986) introduces the notion of a version set consisting of a collection of definitions of a single type. One of the definitions is considered to be the 'current version'. Any object instances are bound to one particular version of a type definition, although varying degrees of compatibility between different versions of a type may exist.

User interface

A database system is a key component of many organizations. Indeed, some organizations view the support of the decision-making process of the company as analogous to the development, operation, and maintenance of the corporate database system. In these circumstances, a great deal of effort is involved in ensuring the correctness of that data, both in terms of the internal integrity of the data, and external security of access to that data. Similarly, the database administrators are continually monitoring the database in an attempt to identify inefficiencies (in any of the normal database activities) and to effect changes to address those inefficiencies.

An important component in all of these areas is the database user interface. Typically, it is at the interface level that much of the confusion arises, leading to inefficient use of the database system, and the issuing of incorrect commands which may not affect the database in the way anticipated by the user. This is particularly true in large, complex applications with a wide variety of different classes of end user. Many object-oriented database system applications typically fall into this latter category.

Until very recently, most commercial database systems offered little more than an *ad hoc* query language as their user interface, usually embedded within a conventional programming language. In the past few years, however, as high-powered, bit-mapped workstations have become more commonplace, users are much more interested in the use of an application development environment providing tools to help in the construction of large, complex database applications (Maier and Zdonik, 1990).

Computer-assisted software engineering (CASE) tools (McClure, 1989) provide some of the most recent advances in database user interfaces. Typically, graphical facilities are provided for schema design and development using a notation such as entity–relationship modelling. The resultant schema can be browsed and, in a small number of cases, also queried.

In object-oriented databases, the schema will often be more complex, involve an extensive network of types, and be extensible. Hence, graphical facilities for schema design, browsing, and query are even more necessary. One of the first systems to provide a graphical schema browsing facility is the Iris system (Fishman, 1989).

However, a number of open issues still remain (Maier and Zdonik, 1990). In particular, while graphical schema browsing facilities are commonly available, little work has looked at graphical schema querying. Also, how can a graphical database interface best be designed for browsing databases containing a very large number of objects, possibly of many different object types?

3.3.2   System functions

Thus far, the object-oriented database characteristics that have been identified and discussed in this chapter have been exclusively in the area of data modelling. We can think of the data modelling aspects as addressing the primary purpose of the database system. However, a vital secondary function is to provide mechanisms for secure, robust, concurrent access to data. In this section we examine approaches to providing these services within object-oriented database systems.

In looking at such mechanisms, it is vital to keep in mind the applications which provide the main catalyst for object-oriented database work: computer-aided design applications such as software engineering environments. The requirements for, and characteristics of, these applications (as reviewed in Chapter 1) have an important effect on the system functions provided.

Transactions

If a transaction is considered to be the unit of database consistency, then a typical transaction in a business data processing application, such as removing money from one bank account and placing it into another, is of short duration, requires only a few database records, and occurs atomically in the sense that the complete transaction either takes place, or it fails and the data is unchanged (i.e. the transaction is 'rolled-back'). While the database is checked for consistency at transaction boundaries, during the execution of a transaction it must be possible to pass through inconsistent states while moving from one consistent pre-transaction state to another consistent post-transaction state. For example, if a transaction consists of removing money from one person's bank account and subsequently depositing the money into another person's account, then at some point during the transaction the money will have been removed from one account without yet having been deposited into the other. If the account balances were summed at that point then that money would seemingly have been lost. Transaction integrity uses the notion of a transaction as the unit of database consistency to ensure that when this situation arises it is invisible to the normal end-user (Date, 1986).

However, it is *not* envisaged that business data processing activities will provide the main application area for object-oriented databases. Design activities such as CAD will be much more typical of an object-oriented database application, with the consequence that it is not always convenient to model end-user interaction with the database in the above way. In fact, the notion of a transaction in a design application can be very different to a business data processing application, exhibiting the following characteristics:

- They are 'conversational', requiring frequent interaction between end user and the database system before completion. For example, a transaction to produce a design specification for a system from an existing requirements document may involve the user in producing a diagram in a particular design notation. Frequent interaction with a set of diagram tools may be required before a satisfactory, and valid, design diagram has been produced.

- They may last for many hours. For example, in producing the design diagram mentioned above, user interaction may extend over several days. In fact, the complete design and implementation of a software system may be considered as one long database transaction which never completes (due to on-going maintenance).

- They may use many records, as the objects accessed may be complex and highly interrelated. A typical design session may involve the user looking through a requirements document, referring to notes on how to produce valid designs in a particular notation, examining previous designs which were produced for related products, and so on.

- They could be non-atomic. The concept of atomicity (i.e. that the whole of a transaction must be committed, or none of it) may not be very applicable to design activities, as undoing a transaction in this environment may remove many hours of work. Confidence in a support environment may be lost if analysts find that a system design they have been working on for a week has been rolled-back to recover database consistency after a system error !

It must be expected, therefore, that for cooperative design activities, information will be shared before the completion of a design transaction. Hence, in some instances the traditional notion of *serializability* as a correctness criterion for concurrently executing transactions may be too restrictive, as it insists that concurrent execution of transactions must produce results that are equivalent to some serial execution of those transactions. This precludes data sharing during transaction execution. As a result, many object-oriented database systems extend the traditional notion of a transaction to address some (or all) of the above characteristics. This can be achieved by either replacing the traditional transaction model with one more appropriate to design activities, or by attempting to build a higher level mechanism on top of an existing transaction model. This latter case is particularly interesting, introducing the concept of a design transaction (sometimes called a *saga*) as a sequence of traditional transactions managed at a higher level of abstraction (Joseph *et al.*, 1989).

We shall further examine the concept of design transactions in the context of three of their principal features: the provision of concurrency control, the maintenance of integrity, and the control of recovery following system failure.

Concurrency

Whenever concurrent, multiple access to shared data is possible, some form of concurrency control must be implemented to prevent data corruption by interference. In a commercial database the control technique most commonly used is known as *locking*, whereby a request for a data object sets a locking flag to say that the object is in use. Conflicting requests for that object are then denied until the lock holder releases the object, resetting the locking flag. This technique may be extended by introducing different classes of lock (e.g. write locks and read locks).

However, this simple technique is of limited use in a design application where a large number of objects may need to be locked in one particular design session, which may take many hours to complete. Hence, it may not be sensible for other designers to wait for the object to be released before they are allowed to proceed with their work. Other methods must therefore be used, taking advantage of the fact that most design objects are developed independently, and are shared at controlled points during the design process (Katz, 1984).

One approach that has been taken can be thought of as a more optimistic approach to concurrency control. If we assume, for example, that it is rare for two designers to amend the same document simultaneously, then we may decide to relax the usual locking approach since it appears too heavy handed, and try to resolve conflicts if and when they arise. For example, in one approach (Bhateja and Katz, 1987) two users are allowed access to the same object, with information sent to each user to make him/her aware of the possibility of conflict. It is the responsibility of the designers to ensure that inconsistencies do not arise.

Much greater concurrency is possible if we also introduce the notion of multiple object versions. Then, access to an object will be to a particular object version. Hence, many users can simultaneously access multiple versions of the object without conflict. If changes to an object no longer modify the current object, but instead create a new version of that object, then it is possible for one user to amend a version of an object while many others are currently reading that version. Note, however, that if two users attempt to amend the same object version concurrently, there is still the possibility of conflict.

Hence, a number of object-oriented database systems handle concurrency using a 'check-in/check-out' approach. When a user wishes to change an object, a version of that object is 'checked-out' into the user's private workspace. This effectively sets a write-lock on that version of the object, disabling other users from attempting to change that version. Once the changes have been made, the user 'checks-in' the object, which creates a new object version. The DAMOKLES system is a good example of this approach (Dittrich *et al.*, 1987).

One final approach to supporting concurrency in an object-oriented database is to try to make concurrency type-specific (Maier and Zdonik, 1990). In this approach, the system takes advantage of the semantics of a user-defined type in controlling concurrency. For example, if two transactions are attempting to access the same queue object concurrently, there may be no conflict if one attempts to remove an item from the front of the queue while the other is adding an item to the end of the queue. By understanding the semantics of the queue type, the system could permit these two transactions to execute in parallel.

Of course, type-specific concurrency control raises many issues which are not as yet fully resolved. For example, aborting a transaction by re-writing the original object may remove concurrent changes. Some more complex form of transaction 'undo' mechanism is required.

Integrity

The tentative and iterative nature of the design process leads to a conversational style of database interaction. Integrity rules have a much more important role in this environment, and can be used to verify a design throughout this interaction, and hence influence a design's development. Hence, in addition to the database-initiated integrity checking described earlier, design applications also have a requirement for a *user-initiated* integrity checking mechanism.

Consider the design of some software component in a large software system. An initial design attempt could be an abstract description of the component using a high-level design language, or some graphical notation. At this point it is useful to perform some basic form of integrity checking to validate the overall design, as early detection of design faults is a vital service. The feedback from these checks will help decide how to continue the design and where to focus attention, promoting a structured approach to the design process by encouraging incremental development. In this way the design continues, slowly being developed and validated until a final design is produced which can be more rigorously checked before allowing others to make use of it.

Such a situation requires a flexible arrangement of integrity checking linked to the transaction boundaries. In particular, it must be possible during a transaction to relax some integrity checks while applying others. The checks can often be divided into two groups: those which are never allowed to be broken (for example, checks which ensure the fundamental integrity of the data model), and those which may validly be broken within a transaction.

The importance of integrity rules is clear, but it may not be obvious what to do when any of the rules are violated. The choice appears to lie between:

- rejecting the offending data and only allowing it to be recorded in the database when it has been amended to pass the checks (however, if a design transaction has taken many hours, then it may not be appropriate to reject the transaction when it attempts to commit due to the failure of some integrity check); and

- allowing the data to stand, but having some form of warning to let other users know that the data has not been fully validated.

As there will be occasions when the integrity rules will need to be violated, usually when a design is incomplete, it is useful to be able to apply each of these methods as appropriate.

Recovery

The long lifetime of design transactions means that traditional approaches to database recovery based on transaction boundaries could result in a great deal of work being lost when a transaction failure occurs. Two mechanisms can be introduced to help.

First, decomposing a transaction into a number of smaller *nested* transactions may help. Then, recovery can be linked to much smaller units of work at the subtransaction boundaries. The model proposed by Korth and Roth (1989) uses nested transactions as the basis of recovery.

Second, recovery within design transactions can be implemented using a *savepoint* technique. At a number of points throughout a transaction (either system defined, or user defined) the changes made since the last savepoint are recorded. In the event of system failure a transaction can be restored to the last savepoint. However, even this technique may lead to significant loss of data unless savepoints are frequent. The DAMOKLES system (Dittrich *et al.*, 1987) adopts a savepoint technique to transaction recovery.

3.3.3   Implementation considerations

Implementation considerations are important because a crucial issue in any database application is *performance*. If database operations are not carried out within a reasonable time, the system falls into disrepute and is not used. In this section we briefly examine some of the main implementation issues which affect object-oriented database performance.

Architecture

Most object-oriented database systems (and, indeed, database systems in general) are implemented as logical database shells requesting data from underlying storage managers. This approach has the advantage of divorcing low-level physical data management and storage considerations from their higher level interpretation and use.

In an object-oriented database system, the storage manager, or *object server*, is responsible for the allocation of disk space to objects, placement of objects on the disk, and so on. The higher level system interprets user operations within the constraints of a particular data model, converting them to requests for particular objects, which it issues to the object server. The Encore system (Skarra *et al.*, 1986) and POSTGRES (Stonebraker, 1986) are two very clear examples of this architectural approach.

An interesting issue is the allocation of services between the higher level shell and the object server. The Encore system, for example, uses ObServer as its object server. This maintains minimal semantics about the objects it stores, treating them essentially as uninterpreted blocks of storage. On the other hand, the GemStone storage manager (Bretl *et al.*, 1989) records information about the internal structure and some of the semantics of the objects it stores (type information, etc.). While the ObServer approach provides a much more neutral storage manager capable of being used as the basis of many different higher level interpreters, the GemStone approach means that the storage manager can make use of the extra information it has in performing disk storage allocation, object retrieval, and so on.

Another architectural issue in this context is the identification of objects within both components of the system. For example, the object server may identify objects using physical disk addresses, while the high-level interpreter uses its own logical object identifiers. If two distinct object references are maintained, then the mapping between the two must be recorded, and object de-referencing must take place when an object moves to/from the object server. This might degrade performance and introduce a potential bottleneck into the system. In the G-Base system, it is claimed that the time taken to perform the mapping of logical to physical object identifiers dominates the disk read/write time (Joseph *et al.*, 1989). However, if the internal physical address is used in both components, physical data independence is lost with the result that changing the storage allocation of an object is no longer an object server issue, but may have profound effects in the high-level interpreter.

Object clustering and caching

The tendency for database schemas in design applications to involve many different data types, associated in a complex network of relationships, means that a single operation on the database may affect many different data types. Existing database systems usually cluster the data on disk on a per data type basis. For example, the tuples of a relation may occupy consecutive disk blocks in order that a single disk read will fetch many or all the tuples of a relation into main memory. Hence, while accessing all the tuples in a relation can take place without further disk operations, collating data from a number of data types can be an expensive operation. This can have a great effect on the performance of design applications.

Furthermore, the problems with excessive disk accesses is exacerbated when the highly structured data items typical of design applications are represented in a data model with a simple set of structuring primitives. For example, in the relational model the complex nature of a design document could be modelled explicitly by defining a number of relations representing the document, document sections, and paragraphs of text within those sections. However, typical operations on documents will require access to all of these relations, involving significant performance overheads with conventional database clustering techniques.

A great deal of work is taking place to examine possible approaches to the clustering of objects on disk as this will significantly affect performance. In particular, both static and dynamic clustering mechanisms are possible. In the static approach the decision about data clustering is taken only once, when an object is created. Dynamic clustering, however, allows the objects to be re-clustered at a later date. In the Cactis system (Hudson and King, 1986), for example, statistics about object retrieval patterns are collected, and reorganization of the clustering of data on disk takes place to suit these patterns, speeding up overall performance. Prefetching is also carried out by attempting to read into main memory all objects likely to be of use before those objects have been referenced.

Handling large objects

Computer-aided design applications may require significantly large amounts of data to be recorded. In fact, it is possible that a single object may itself be very large, perhaps larger than the host computer's main memory. Thus, techniques must be implemented for subdividing large objects in a controlled fashion, allowing individual pieces of an object to be examined and used.

The EXODUS system has particularly addressed itself to the problems of handling large objects (Carey *et al.*, 1986). The EXODUS storage manager implements a novel object storage algorithm which essentially allows arbitrarily large objects to be stored without significant overhead in reading/writing components of a large object.

Distribution

It is likely that large computer-aided design applications will be implemented by a distributed group of engineers. Hence, object-oriented database systems must expect to function in a distributed computer environment. While research into conventional distributed database mechanisms is already well advanced, the many differences in characteristics which we have discussed have led object-oriented database system researchers to investigate new approaches to distributed object management. For performance reasons, and because it more directly fits the co-operative style of interaction of a design activity, most object-oriented database systems concentrate on supporting a federated collection of databases rather than attempting to implement a truly distributed database system.[1]

Distributed object management is still in its infancy, with simple, pragmatic solutions currently being adopted. In G-Base, for example, limited distributed capabilities are provided by implementing an interface between G-Base and the Oracle relational database system (Joseph *et al.*, 1989).

3.4   SUMMARY

In this chapter we have provided an overview of object-oriented database systems by reviewing the requirements they are attempting to fulfil, examining their basic characteristics, and describing many of the issues which are being addressed to make object-oriented database technology a practical reality. In particular, the object-oriented concepts identified in the previous chapter were reviewed in the context of object-oriented database systems. A number of important issues which arose as a consequence of supporting these concepts were then analysed.

Armed with this background, the next chapter provides an overview of a number of example object-oriented database systems: GemStone, Iris, and ONTOS. By examining these systems we are able to pull together many of the concepts discussed in this chapter into the coherent framework of particular system implementations, and present a review of the current state of object-oriented database products.

---

[1] We distinguish a *federated* collection of databases as a group of independent database systems with controlled communication between them. In contrast, a *distributed* database is one in which a set of databases is managed by a single global schema, participating in distributed transactions.

4

A REVIEW OF SELECTED OBJECT-ORIENTED DATABASES

Any description of object-oriented databases is rather dry without providing an overview of some existing systems. However, rather than attempting to examine all available database systems which can be classified as object-oriented, we have selected a small number of systems which we hope will be representative of the state of the art at present.

The systems reviewed are taken from industry to give a feel for the current commercial reality of object-oriented database systems. Of the three systems reviewed, GemStone has been available as a product for a number of years, the first version of ONTOS was released at the end of 1989, while Iris is a research prototype whose results are expected to feed back into future database products at Hewlett-Packard.

To describe these representative systems, we make use of the framework of issues outlined in the previous chapter. In particular, each system is reviewed under the following broad categories:

- *Data model aspects.*   A vital component of an object-oriented database system is the model of data which it embodies. We give examples of the data model by defining a simple database schema and attempting to execute some simple queries against that schema (see below).

- *System functions.*   The basic mechanisms provided for data sharing, integrity, and recovery are described.

- *Implementation considerations.*   Aspects of the database which affect performance of the system are reviewed. This includes architectural issues, object clustering and indexing, and distribution.

To facilitate comparison between the different systems, we can define a simple example schema which we attempt to define and query in each of the three systems. An entity–relationship (E–R) representation of the example schema is shown in

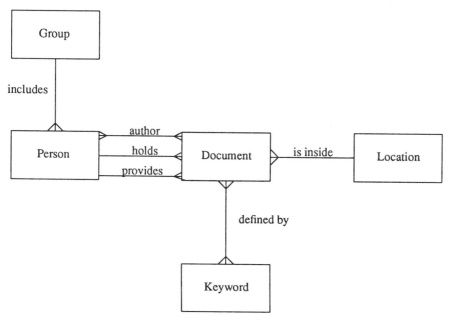

Figure 4.1   An example schema using an E–R notation

Fig. 4.1. This schema should be interpreted as follows:

- Information is recorded about documents such as specifications, test reports, and so on.

- Each document is provided by one person, and may be currently held by one person, but may be authored by many people.

- Each person may belong to a single group.

- Each document has a location; many documents may be stored at a single location.

- A document is defined by a number of keywords. A keyword may apply to many documents in the system.

4.1 GEMSTONE

GemStone is the first product of Servio Logic Corporation in the USA (Maier and Stein, 1987; Penney and Stein, 1987; Bretl *et al.*, 1989). The basic approach taken was to examine the Smalltalk language and system, and to identify a number of requirements with regard to making Smalltalk a database system. The result is the language OPAL, which manipulates persistent data objects controlled by a disk-based storage manager. The basic architecture is illustrated in Fig. 4.2.

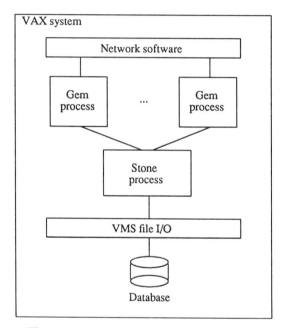

Figure 4.2   The basic GemStone architecture

There are two main components to the architecture.

1. *Stone* provides persistent object management, concurrency control, authorization, transaction, and recovery services.

2. *Gem* augments the Stone services by providing compilation mechanisms for OPAL programs, user authorization control, and monitoring of user sessions. In particular, Gem provides the predefined set of OPAL classes and methods which are available in a GemStone system. These are shown in Fig. 4.3, using indentation to indicate the different levels in the class hierarchy.

```
Object
    Association
        SymbolAssociation
    Behaviour
        Class
        Metaclass
    Boolean
    Collection
        SequenceableCollection
            Array
                InvariantArray
                Repository
            String
                InvariantString
                    Symbol
        Bag
            Set
                Dictionary
                    SymbolDictionary
                        LanguageDictionary
                SymbolSet
                UserProfileSet
    CompiledMethod
    Magnitude
        Character
        DateTime
        Number
            Float
            Integer
                SmallInteger
    MethodContext
        Block
            SelectionBlock
    Segment
    Stream
        PositionableStream
            ReadStream
            WriteStream
    System
    UndefinedObject
    UserProfile
```

Figure 4.3   The predefined GemStone class hierarchy

4.1.1 Data model aspects

The OPAL language is heavily influenced by the Smalltalk language. As a result, schema development takes place through users defining classes of objects in many different categories. As seen in Fig. 4.3, an initial class hierarchy is provided including classes for objects, sets, bags, lists, and so on. Thus, a user can define a new object class by extending the existing class hierarchy. Any class which is a subclass of the Object class is considered to be persistent (i.e. its instances persist across application program invocations).

Schema representation

To create 'record types' we must define new classes which are subtypes of the class Object. To do this we send the message *subclass* to the Object class and define the instance variables for that class (we can think of an instance variable as analogous to a field in a record definition). As any class of object can be stored in an instance variable, we add additional constraints to ensure that the instance variables we define store objects of the correct class (i.e. are drawn from the appropriate domain). We use the notation '#[...]' to define an array of instance variables which we can think of as the attributes of the object class.

Hence, we could define the entity types of our example schema as shown in Fig. 4.4.

Note that in Fig. 4.4 we have not represented the relationships which hold between entity types (e.g. the 'Authors' relationship between a document and a person). This is because there are two possible ways in which these relationships can be recorded. Using the 'Authors' relationship as an example, we could define it in either of the following ways:

- By defining a new object class Author which references both Person and Document object classes.

```
Object subclass: 'Author'
    instVarNames: #['doc', 'written-by']
    constraints: #[#[ #doc, Document],
        #[ #written-by, Person]].
```

- Using set-valued attributes we could amend the definition of Document to include an 'author' instance variable. Note also that we need to create a set of objects, which we call PersonSet, and we constrain the elements of that set to be of the class Person. This allows us to make the link between Document and Person by giving Document a set-valued attribute. This models the fact that a document may be authored by a number of people.

```
Object subclass: `Location'
    instVarNames: #[`location-id', `name']
    constraints: #[#[ #location-id, String],
        #[ #name, String]].

Object subclass: `Document'
    instVarNames: #[`document-id', `revision-number',
        `title', `publication-date', `status', `type', `contents']
    constraints: #[#[ #document-id, Integer],
        #[ #revision-number, Integer],
        #[ #title, String],
        #[ #publication-date, Date],
        #[ #status, String],
        #[ #type, String],
        #[ #contents, Text]].

Object subclass: `Person'
    instVarNames: #[`person-id', `name', `code-proj']
    constraints: #[#[ #person-id, Integer],
        #[ #name, String],
        #[ #code-proj, Integer]].

Object subclass: `Group'
    instVarNames: #[`group-id', `name']
    constraints: #[#[ #group-id, Integer],
        #[ #name, String]].

Object subclass: `Keyword'
    instVarNames: #[`keyword']
    constraints: #[#[ #keyword, String]].
```

Figure 4.4   An example schema definition in OPAL

```
Set subclass: PersonSet
   constraints: Person.

Object subclass: Document
   instVarName: #[ ..., 'author']
   constraints: #[ ...
         ...
         ...
         #[ #author, PersonSet]].
```

Manipulation of the information base

Unlike relational database systems, OPAL does not have a predefined algebra of operations. Hence, specific operators must be defined for each different object class by defining appropriate *methods*. For example, if an object class Employee had instance variables 'first' and 'last' recording the forename and last name of an employee, then we could define a method to return the full name of an employee as:

```
method:  Employee
    fullName
        |temp|
        temp := first
        temp := temp + ' ' + last
        ^temp
%
```

The method definition for *fullName* defines a temporary variable 'temp' which is assigned the value of the instance variable 'first'. Then, 'temp' is extended by concatenating a space and the value of the instance variable 'last'. Finally, the value of 'temp' is returned as the result of the message *fullName* through the statement '^temp'.

In fact, having said that no predefined algebra exists, each of the predefined OPAL classes does have a number of methods available which are inherited by any subclasses that a user defines. For example, the Set class has a method 'select' which retrieves members of a set based on a predicate. A message to invoke the method has the general form:

```
select:  [:X | <code involving X which returns true or false>]
```

When a message of this form is sent to an object O which is a subclass of Set, it has the effect of returning a new object (also a subclass of Set) that is the set of all objects in O for which the body of the select operation returns true. For example, suppose we wish to retrieve all documents with the status 'Approved'. If the object `Documents` is a set of `Document` objects and has members consisting of objects representing all documents known to the system, then we could write the query as:

```
ApprovedDocs := Documents  select:
                      [:d | (d getStatus) = 'Approved']
```

The message *getStatus* returns the status of each document, and if that value is 'Approved', then the document concerned is made an element of the set `ApprovedDocs`.

As a final query example, consider a request to obtain all documents defined by a given keyword. Let us assume that each document has a list of keywords associated with it via an instance variable 'keywords'. Also, assume the keywords we are searching for are members of the set object `SearchKeywords`. We could create an empty set of documents as:

```
DocsIncludingKeywords := Document new
```

Assuming we have defined an 'insert' method for `DocsIncludingKeywords`, then we could get all the documents using the *do* method which applies a block of code to each element of a given set:

```
SearchKeywords do:
[ :s |

    Documents do:
    [ :d |
        (( d getKeywords) testFor: s )
        ifTrue: [ DocsIncludingKeywords insert: d ]
    ]
]
```

To perform an update operation on any object, we again have to define appropriate methods. For example, to insert details of a new person we could define a new method as:

```
method:  Person
   insertID: id
   insertName: na
   insertCodeProj: cp
     |NewPerson|
```

```
NewPerson := Person new
NewPerson storeID: id; storeName: na; storeCodeProj: cp
Self add: NewPerson
%
```

The method is defined by its parameters 'insertID', 'insertName', and 'insert-CodeProj'. A temporary variable 'NewPerson' is set to be a new Person object, and is assigned appropriate instance variables through the messages *storeID:*, *storeName:*, and *storeCodeProj:*. Finally, the new object is added to the set (i.e. Self is the receiver of the message *add:* with the parameter NewPerson).

Thus, if we wanted to add details of the person named 'Brown' to the set Persons, we would say:

```
Persons  insertId: 99  insertName: 'Brown'  insertCodeProj: 3
```

4.1.2   System functions

Concurrency control

In GemStone, both pessimistic and optimistic concurrency control schemes are implemented, either of which may be used depending on which is more likely to give better performance. Hence, the user decides on which scheme to adopt based on a knowledge of which is most appropriate for the application being developed.

In the optimistic scheme a shadow copy of the user workspace is taken at the start of a transaction. When the transaction commits, a check is made for possible conflicts with other transactions which have committed since this transaction began. In the absence of any conflicts, the shadow copy replaces the original. This approach ensures deadlock can never occur, and has minimum transaction overhead. Of course, when conflicts are detected at commit time, the whole transaction must be rolled back and replayed.

In the pessimistic scheme, a traditional two-phase locking protocol is used.

Security

To provide controlled access to data, GemStone allows different users to have different levels of access to objects. Authorization is based on the notion of a user *segment*. Each user controls at least one segment, and all objects are owned by at least one segment. Authorization is on a per segment basis, with read and write permissions being set for objects held in that segment (analogous to the file permissions of an operating system).

Recovery

The shadow paging technique described above provides the basis of recovery control in GemStone. In particular, the shadow pages are only made permanent on transaction commit. Hence, failure of a transaction (or transaction abort) does not require any changes to be undone.

To provide support in the event of media failure such as a disk crash, GemStone allows replication of data through the notion of a *repository*. A special class of object called Repository responds to the message 'replicate'. This maintains two copies of the repository, allowing one to be used as a backup of the other. The system maintains consistency between the two copies. Thus, the user is responsible for requesting multiple copies to allow recovery.

Schema modification

Schema modification primitives are provided so that changes to a class definition can be made with automatic conversion of existing class instances to comply with the new class definition.

4.1.3   Implementation considerations

Object indexing

Collections of OPAL objects may be indexed to speed up associative access to those objects. To allow this GemStone has a facility which it calls *indexed associative access* (Servio Logic Corporation, 1989). This allows indexing of data objects for retrieval by name or by value.

As an example, suppose we wish to create an index on the object MyDocs which is a set of Document objects. We could then execute the command:

```
MyDocs createEqualityIndexOn: 'title'
```

This creates an index on the instance variable 'title' for the set of documents MyDocs.

To retrieve all documents with the title 'A Good Title', we would normally write a query in OPAL which has the form:

```
MyDocs select:
    [ :aDoc | aDoc.title = 'A Good Title' ]
```

However, to make use of any indices on the paths used, the user must explicitly replace the square brackets with curly ones:

```
MyDocs select:
    { :aDoc | aDoc.title = 'A Good Title' }
```

Note, however, that it is the user who must request an index to be maintained. Then, a different querying syntax may be used to take advantage of the index. As a consequence, physical data independence is reduced. For example, if we decide to delete the request for an index on MyDocs, the result will be that any later operations which use that index will now have to be amended.

Large objects

Support for large persistent objects is provided so that one object can span many physical disk pages. Transparent to the user, such an object is manipulated by bringing only a subset of the pages into a user workspace at any one time. This is possible because large objects are maintained as a tree structure of smaller pages.

4.2 IRIS

The Iris database system (Fishman, 1989; Lyngbaek and Kent, 1986) is a research prototype under development at Hewlett-Packard Laboratories in Palo Alto. One of the most interesting features of the Iris system is the evolutionary approach that is being taken. As illustrated in Fig. 4.5, the Iris database consists of an *object manager* which is built on top of a relational database system (Allbase) which acts as the *storage manager* for the system. This design has a number of advantages.

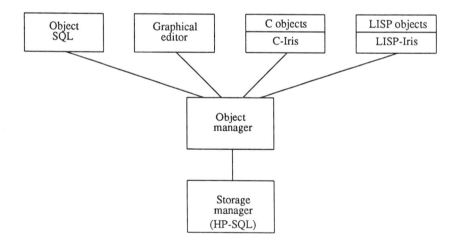

Figure 4.5   The basic Iris architecture

In particular, all Iris queries and functions are converted into an intermediate form of extended relational algebra. It is at this level that query optimization can take place based on conventional algebraic techniques.

4.2.1   Data model aspects

The Iris object manager supports an object-oriented data model, providing facilities for schema definition, data manipulation, and query processing. These facilities are accessed through a number of different interfaces. In addition to embedded C and LISP interfaces, a graphical interface and an (extended) SQL interface have been provided. The latter interface is particularly interesting, as it has been based on extending the SQL language towards object-based manipulation. The result is a language called *Object-SQL (OSQL)* (Beech, 1988). As it has many similarities to the basic SQL language, users of Iris should have few problems in moving to it from traditional relational database systems which use SQL. Similarly, it may be possible to convert many existing applications from relational databases to Iris without undue effort.

The OSQL language extends SQL in three main ways:

1. *Object identity.*   Every object is given a unique, system-generated identifier. The system does not explicitly reveal identifier values. However, end users can make use of these identifiers as unique object handles. In particular, direct reference can be made to objects rather than using attribute values drawn from common domains to indicate relationships between different entities. The use of direct object references automatically enforces some aspects of referential integrity.

2. *User-defined functions.*   It is possible for end users to define their own functions on data and then use those functions within queries. A function can be defined extensionally (by explicitly defining the result of the query for particular input parameters) or intensionally (by writing a query as the body of the function).

3. *Syntactic changes.*   A number of syntactic changes to the language are made to try to enforce a new way of thinking about the language. For example, `create table` is replaced by `create type`. (Iris uses the term *type* where GemStone uses the term *class*.)

In addition to the ability to allow users to define new types, Iris has a predefined set of types, as shown in Fig. 4.6. Any user-defined types (such as `Person`) are automatically inserted into the type hierarchy as direct subtypes of `UserTypeObject`. By inserting the clause `Subtype of` into a `create type` statement, the type hierarchy can be extended.

```
Object
    Type
        UserType
    ArgRes
        Argument
        Result
    Function
    Literal
        Integer
        Real
        Boolean
        String
    UserTypeObject
```

Figure 4.6   The predefined Iris type hierarchy

Schema representation

The entity types of our example schema in Fig. 4.1 may be defined in OSQL as shown in Fig. 4.7.

As with the OPAL example, Fig. 4.7 defines the entity types, but not the relationships between those entity types. The OSQL model provides the flexibility to record those relationships in three different ways:

1. As relationship types, linking together independent entity types. For example, the Author relationship could be defined by a new type definition with appropriate attributes.

```
create type Author
(
    doc Document,
    written-by Person
);
```

Notice that referential integrity is automatically enforced due to the fact that direct references to the appropriate type are made, not their underlying domain. This is possible as a result of the object identity principle described earlier.

2. As set-valued attributes. For example, the Author relationship could be held as a set-valued attribute of Document.

```
create type Location
(
   location-id char(10) required unique,
   name char(20)
);

create type Document
(
   document-id integer required unique,
   revision-number integer required unique,
   title char(50),
   publication-date date,
   status char(10),
   type char(10),
   contents text
);

create type Person
(
   person-id integer required unique,
   name char(20),
   code-proj integer
);

create type Group
(
   group-id integer required unique,
   name char(20)
);

create type Keyword
(
   keyword char(20) required unique
);
```

Figure 4.7   An example schema definition in OSQL

```
create type Document
(
    ...
    author set of Person
);
```

This approach makes queries to find all the authors of a document very easy. However, the inverse query, to find all documents written by a given author will require each document to be retrieved and the set of authors for that document examined.

3. As user-defined functions. For example, the Author relationship could be defined as a function which, given a document identifier, returns the set of authors of that document.

```
create function authorOf(Document) --> set of Person;
```

The main body of the function can be defined in a number of different ways. These are discussed later in this section.

Note, however, that this approach suffers from the same disadvantage as the one above, and an inverse function 'hasAuthors' would need to be defined to obtain a list of authors for a given document.

This flexibility of OSQL means that the most 'natural' representation of relationships can be chosen, aiding user comprehension of the schema and speeding up access for some kinds of queries (though often at the expense of others).

Manipulation of the information base

To define queries against the schema, OSQL uses a modified form of the SQL 'select' statement. For example, to list the identifiers, version numbers, and titles of all documents we could have:

```
select document-id, version-number, title
for each Document;
```

This query has the effect of examining each instance of the type Document, and retrieving the attributes specified.

A more complex query might be to find all the documents for a given set of keywords. We would have different queries depending on which of the three possible representations described above had been chosen to represent the 'defined by' relationship between Document and Keyword.

For the first option, a new type DefinedBy could be defined as:

```
create type DefinedBy as
(
    adoc Document
    haskey Keyword
);
```

Then, a query to find all documents which have any of the keywords recorded as instances of the type SearchKeys (which has a single attribute 'key') could be written as:

```
select title(d)
for each Document d, DefinedBy b, SearchKeys k
where key(k) = haskey(b) and d = adoc(b)
```

In this query, the uniqueness property of objects means that variables can be used within the query (such as 'd' and 'k') and may be bound to the objects retrieved. The query is interpreted as retrieving a keyword 'k' from SearchKeys and matching it with a DefinedBy object 'b'. Then, the title of the corresponding Document object 'd' is retrieved.

The second option requires that Document has a set-valued attribute, 'keywords', which holds a list of keywords which are applied to each document. Then, assuming that the desired keywords are the instances of the type SearchKeys with single attribute 'key':

```
select document-id, version-number
for each Document d, SearchKeys k
where key(k) in keywords(d);
```

In this example each of the keywords in SearchKeys is checked against the set of keywords defined for a document.

In the third option, if we had represented the 'defined by' relationship as a function, we could have defined the function definedBy as:

```
create function definedBy(Document) --> set of Keywords;
```

We could then *extensionally* define the function definedBy by explicitly recording the keywords attached to each document. For example, if document 'd1' is defined by the keywords 'database' and 'object-oriented', we could write:

```
set definedBy(d1) = 'database';
add definedBy(d1) = 'object-oriented';
```

We could then write a query to find all documents defined by the keyword 'database' as:

```
select title
for each Document d
where 'database' in definedBy(d);
```

As a final example, we consider update operations in OSQL. To add details of a new person, for example, we could write:

```
create Person(person-id, name, code-proj)
instances brown( 6, 'Brown', 2 ),
          jones( 7, 'Jones', 2 ),
          smith( 8, 'Smith', 3 );
```

This creates three new instances of `Person`, attaching a variable name ('brown', 'jones', and 'smith') to each one to act as unique handles on those objects for the duration of that session.

Instead of being defined extensionally, an OSQL function can be defined *intensionally* as a database query, or as a piece of code in a programming language such as C:

- Intensional functions are defined by using a 'select' operation as the body of a function definition. For example, if the type `Document` has an attribute 'authors' recording the set of authors of a document, then we could define a function to return all the documents authored by a given person as:

```
create function authorsDocs(Person p) --> set of Documents
   as select
       each Document d
       where p in authors(d);
```

- For computational completeness, functions may also be implemented in a programming language such as C. These are called *foreign functions*. This greatly increases the flexibility of Iris, allowing users to define their own storage structures for specialized applications for example.

Note also that predicates may be defined by creating functions which do not return a result. For example, to restrict keywords to some relevant subset, we could write:

```
create function Relevant(Keyword);
```

We could then extensionally define the keywords which are considered relevant to this application.

4.2.2   System functions

Iris provides simple version control facilities. Any user-defined object can be made versionable, and can then only be accessed through *checkout* and *checkin* commands which create the next version of the object. Controlled sharing of versions requires the user to define explicitly a lock when checking out a version.

Many of the basic database management facilities (such as transactions, recovery, indexing, and locking) are not explicitly defined for Iris, but are available through using the relational database system Allbase as the underlying storage manager. Hence, Iris inherits these existing services from Allbase.

However, recognizing the limitations of these services in the context of support for design applications, the Iris project is investigating extensions to the basic storage manager to provide support for long-lived transactions and transactions which require access to large numbers of database objects.

4.2.3   Implementation considerations

Again, having concentrated on providing the functionality of the object-oriented data model, the Iris project is only now turning its attention towards performance issues such as object clustering and indexing.

4.3   ONTOS

In 1987 Ontologic produced an object-oriented database system called VBase (Andrews and Harris, 1987). Two distinct language interfaces were provided for VBase:

1. TDL (type definition language) was for specifying the data model: defining the data types and their operators.

2. COP (C object processor), a superset of the C language, was for implementing operators and for writing application programs.

However, while VBase aroused a great deal of interest, Ontologic found that there was widespread resistance to learning 'yet another programming language'. That, coupled with performance difficulties, led Ontologic to redesign their system completely to produce a second generation product. Originally called VBase+, then renamed OB2, this new product has recently been renamed *ONTOS*. The rest of this review refers to ONTOS, initially released towards the end of 1989.

The aim of ONTOS is to provide a persistent object store for C++ programs (Ontologic Inc., 1988; Ontologic Inc., 1989; Andrews *et al.*, 1989). Hence, rather than having to learn a new programming language, ONTOS users write programs in the C++ programming language, augmented by operations to open the database, start transactions, and so on. A library of C++ classes is predefined, which allows programs to invoke operators to create persistent objects, retrieve and store objects in a database, and to start and commit (or abort) transactions. The predefined class hierarchy is given in Fig. 4.8.

Any ONTOS object which is an instance of the class `Object` (or any of its subclasses) is a persistent data object. Users can create instances of the predefined classes and also extend the set of persistent classes at runtime, with the system taking responsibility for runtime checking of operator arguments and operator invocation.

Thus, a typical ONTOS application program defines a set of (persistent) class definitions, makes calls to the operators that have been specified in the predefined or user-defined class definitions, and also *activates* and *deactivates* database objects.

The ONTOS notion of activating an object is the process of transferring it from a database into the application program, and hence making it accessible to the C++ structures and operators. The effect of this is to bring the object into main memory and to convert the object identifier into a main memory pointer, making subsequent access to that object much faster.[1] Deactivation is the inverse operation, copying the object from main memory to the persistent database. Objects can also be assigned names, and it is through their names that most access to objects is made.

4.3.1   Data model aspects

To develop a database application in ONTOS, the user writes an application program in C++, including the definition and manipulation of persistent C++ classes. ONTOS automatically maintains a unique object identifier for each persistent object that is created. Hence, in addition to defining data properties for an object class, links between classes can be modelled by referencing the identifiers of other objects. To make such a link, one of two possible approaches may be taken:

1. *A transparent reference.*   In most cases, to represent a link between objects a transparent reference would be made. This involves a level of indirection, and when a user requests access to a referenced object, the system automatically checks to see if that object is currently active. If not, it is activated by the system and brought into main memory. For example, if a `Person` object references a `Department` object representing a person being a member of a particular department, we could define the link using a transparent reference, or `TRef`, as:

---

[1] This conversion of object identifiers to main memory pointers, sometimes called *pointer swizzling*, is a time-consuming operation. Some of the problems of pointer swizzling are discussed in Joseph *et al.*(1989).

```
CleanupObj
      Entity
            Real
            String
            Integer
            Failure
            ExceptionHandler
             Object
                  Aggregate
                        Set
                        List
                        Association
                              Dictionary
                              Array
                  Type
                        PropertyType
                        Procedure
                  ArgumentList
                  ArgumentListIterator
                  ArgSpec
                  Directory
```

Figure 4.8   The predefined ONTOS class hierarchy

```
class Person public : Entity
{
   TRef* inDept;
   ...
}
```

When a user attempts to obtain information about the department of a a particular Person object, the user does not need to check to see if the appropriate Department object has already been activated. The system will perform this check automatically, activating the object if necessary.

Hence, references are most often defined as pointers to the class TRef. When a user wishes to access a referenced object (e.g. a person's department), the user must use the function 'binding()' which obtains the actual pointer to the object referenced. (An inverse function 'FindTRef()' converts a direct pointer to an object to a TRef pointer.)

In the ONTOS literature (Ontologic Inc., 1989; Andrews *et al.*, 1989) it is strongly recommended that users represent links between objects as transparent references as they free the user from having to keep track of which objects have been 'activated' and which have not.

2. *A direct reference.*   To avoid the overhead of transparent references, a direct reference to an object can be made. In this case, when a user activates an object any inactive objects which it references are not fetched by the system. Instead, such references are set to the default value Inactive. Hence, it is the user's responsibility to keep track of which objects are currently active. The example of a person referencing their department would now be written as a direct reference to a Department object:

```
class Person public : Entity
{
    Department* inDept;
    ...
}
```

Schema representation

For each of the database entity types we wish to model, we must define an appropriate persistent C++ class. For each class we give the class name, the parent class in the class hierarchy, and a set of attributes. To access individual attribute values of an object we can impose a protocol on the class definitions which ensures that the only way to retrieve or update the attribute values is via a set of 'accessor' functions. For example, for an attribute 'X', we explicitly define a function to read the value of 'X' and another to write the value of 'X'. As we can overload function names in C++, we can give both functions the same name. The read function has no parameters and returns the attribute's value, while the write function is given the value to be written to the attribute as a parameter and returns void.

Hence, using the protocol described above, we could define the entity types for our example schema as shown in Fig. 4.9.

For the relationships which hold between the entity types, we have a number of choices to make. First, whether to use transparent or direct references between classes, as discussed earlier. For our example we shall choose transparent references.

Second, there are two possible ways to make a link between objects when there is a many-to-many relationship between object types.

1. We can create a new object class to represent the relationship. For example, for the 'authors' relationship between people and documents, we could define a class Authors as:

```
class Authors : public Entity
{
    TRef* aPerson;
    TRef* aDocument;
    ...
};
```

2. We can create a new object class representing sets of authors, and add an attribute to Document which references such an object. For example:

```
class AuthorSet : public Set
{
};
class Document : public Entity
{
    ...
    TRef* hasAuthors;

    public:
    AuthorSet* authors()
        { return (AuthorSet*)hasAuthors -> binding();}

    void authors(AuthorSet* someAuthors)
        { hasAuthors = someAuthors -> FindTRef();}
    ...
};
```

Hence, we would create a new AuthorSet object containing the appropriate authors, and link that set to a document.

Manipulating the information base

So far we have only discussed access to individual attribute values of an object (accessor functions). ONTOS does not have a general query language, and so to obtain any information from the classes defined we would have to specify the appropriate operation for each query. If it were thought useful enough, we could define the query as a new function within the class definition which could then be used in the same way as the accessor functions. Otherwise, we could define the query as a set of statements in the application program.

For example, to obtain all documents with a status of 'Approved' we could define a set of Document objects called AllDocs to represent all the documents known to the system. A set iterator would allow us to cycle through the documents to print

```
class Location : public Entity
{
    char* locationId;
    char* locationName;

    public:

    virtual int LocId() { return locationId; }
    virtual void LocId(char* newLocationId);

    virtual int LocName() { return locationName; }
    virtual void LocName(char* newLocationName);
};

class Document : public Entity
{
    int documentId;
    int revisionNo;
    char* title;
    int pubDate;
    char* status;
    char* type;
    char* contents;

    public:

    virtual int DocId() { return documentId; }
    virtual void DocId(char* newDocumentId);
    ...
};
```

```
class Keyword : public Entity
{
   char* keyName;

   public:

   virtual int key() { return keyName; }
   virtual void key(char* newKeyName);
};

class Person : public Entity
{
   int    personId;
   char*  personName;
   int    codeProj;

   public:

   virtual int Id() { return personId; }
   virtual void Id(char* newPersonId);
   ...
};

class Group : public Entity
{
   int groupId;
   char* groupName;

   public:

   virtual int groupId() { return groupId; }
   virtual void groupId(char* newGroupId);
   ...
};
```

Figure 4.9   An example schema definition in ONTOS

out their title if they have an 'Approved' status:

```
SetIterator theDocs( AllDocs );
Document* aDoc;

while (aDoc = theDocs())
   if (aDoc->status() == 'Approved')
      cout << aDoc->title();     \\ print out the title
```

In this example, a set iterator 'theDocs' is defined for the set AllDocs. Then, using this set iterator each of the documents in AllDocs is retrieved and the status value tested. If it is set to 'Approved', then the title is retrieved and printed.

4.3.2   System functions

ONTOS supports transactions by supplying special functions to start, commit, and abort transactions. A pessimistic transaction mechanism is employed, with locking at the object level. While a number of default conflict resolution actions have been defined by the system, on starting a transaction, a user-defined function can be supplied to implement the appropriate action to take when transaction conflicts arise. For example, when activation or deactivation operations conflict, the user may decide to abort the transaction, or to wait and repeat the offending operation.

In addition, transactions may be arbitrarily nested in order to divide large transactions into smaller ones which are less likely to cause conflicts. A number of visibility and access rules have been defined to control changes to objects in a nested transaction in relation to its enclosing parent transaction.

4.3.3   Implementation considerations

Architecture

ONTOS is based on a client/server architecture. This facilitates distribution of the object base over a network of machines, with interprocess communication and shared memory services provided. As illustrated in Fig. 4.10, a number of databases may be registered as servers to the client. The application accesses the persistent database objects through the facilities of the client (i.e. the predefined class hierarchy).

Object clustering

Both activation and deactivation may take place on single objects, or on groups of objects. Three functions are provided for object activation:

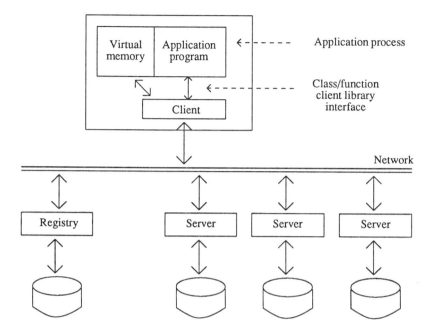

Figure 4.10   The basic ONTOS client/server architecture

1. *VB_getObject.*   This activates the single object whose name is given as a parameter.

2. *VB_getCluster.*   A group of objects may form a cluster and be activated using a single operation. This is useful for manipulating a set of objects which are logically related.

3. *VB_getClosure.*   Of particular importance to engineering applications is the ability to manipulate an object together with all the objects it references (e.g. a parts explosion). The closure of an object represents all the persistent objects it points to, forming a graph of objects. Rather than the user having to keep track of all the objects in such a closure, a single closure operation may be used.

The inverse operations *VB_putObject*, *VB_putCluster*, and *VB_putClosure* are also available allowing a single object, cluster of objects, or closure of objects to be deactivated (i.e. written to disk).

As related groups of objects can be moved to and from disk in a single fetch or store operation, the granularity of a cluster has an effect on the speed and efficiency of the operations.

Miscellaneous issues

A number of other issues are also worth noting:

1. The ONTOS system is designed to be used with existing C++ translators and compilers, and hence does not need to provide its own. Currently, ONTOS is supported for use with the AT&T (cfront) and Glokenspiel (Designer C++) translators.

2. A set of utilities are provided with ONTOS which help in its use and administration. The main utilities provided are:

    *   an interactive browser for examining and modifying the class definitions;
    *   an enhanced *Make* tool to keep application programs up to date with respect to the class hierarchy;
    *   a set of commands for altering the physical clustering of objects on disk to improve data transfer performance;
    *   a registration facility for defining new users and new nodes in the physical system architecture.

3. A number of further enhancements are planned for future releases. Conversely, the following are facilities which are *not* guaranteed to be included in the first release:

    *   database backup and restore facilities;
    *   transaction logging and recovery;
    *   statistics gathering and reporting utilities;
    *   built-in mechanisms for different levels of data security;
    *   support for multiple versions of objects;
    *   an SQL interface to the object base.

An interesting aside is that the goal of ONTOS is to achieve up to a *500-fold* performance improvement over relational databases for some types of applications.[1] (Presumably this covers support for design data management applications such as integrated project support environments (IPSEs).) The ONTOS designers believe such an improvement is possible owing to the semantic modelling capability of the object model, the ONTOS implementation use of object caching, and the ONTOS object clustering facilities which help improve disk transfer of structured and related objects. However, as yet no figures have been produced to show that ONTOS

---

[1]The argument that object-oriented databases can provide such a level of performance is also supported in Maier(1986).

is even close to achieving this level of performance.

4.4   DISCUSSION

Following our review of three example object-oriented database systems, we now draw out a number of interesting points.

4.4.1   Access to metadata

An important advantage of using a database system for recording data is that the database system records both the end-user data and information about the structure of that data. For example, the database records details of the different categories of data stored, which attributes they have, how the entities are related, and so on.

This information about the structure of the data is called *metadata*. In all three of the object-oriented databases that we examined, it has been shown that schema development is equivalent to extending a predefined class (or type) hierarchy with user-defined classes. This approach means that user-defined data and metadata are both represented in the same way—as instances of classes in the class hierarchy. Hence, both user data and metadata can be accessed (i.e. retrieved) in the same way. This greatly simplifies the database interface.

4.4.2   Modelling flexibility

One of the interesting features of this analysis of object-oriented databases has been a recognition of the flexibility in data modelling provided by object-oriented data models. In the Iris system, for example, relationships between objects could be modelled in three different ways: by defining an associative object linking the related objects, using a set-valued attribute, or by defining an intensional or extensional function.

This choice in representing relationships provides the database designer with greater flexibility in modelling real-world situations. For example, some relationships are more naturally represented as functions as opposed to defining (artificial) associative objects.

In addition, this flexibility allows the user to make better use of the database system in developing large applications (Beech, 1988). For example, when amendments to the schema are required, a large number of changes can be accommodated without affecting existing data by defining new functions to represent additional relationships between objects.

Similarly, it may be possible to create a library of 'standard' class definitions for a project. These definitions can be imported into different database applications, and may be tailored by creating additional set-valued attributes, functions, and so on.

4.4.3   Direct object references

The example systems also show that relationships between objects may be represented as direct object references. This is because the system automatically maintains a unique identifier for every object created. This is in contrast to the relational model, which has well-known problems with its use of attribute values as unique keys for entities (Kent, 1979). Indeed, in many systems, the only way to enforce uniqueness of tuples in a relation is to define explicitly a unique index on the key attribute(s) of the relation.

In addition, relational systems use foreign keys to record links between relations. While the definition of the relational model insists on referential integrity being maintained (i.e. that a foreign key must reference an entity which exists in the database) in practice this rule is rarely directly implemented. Many relational systems have no enforcement of referential integrity constraints, while the better systems often provide extra facilities to allow a user to create referential constraints explicitly. This manual creation of the checks inevitably leads to the possibility of errors and omissions.

4.4.4   Built-in access paths

The advantages of providing alternative ways to represent relationships between objects have been cited above. However, it is important to realize that there are implications to using some of the approaches. For example, if a relationship is held as a set-valued attribute, a preferred method of access to that information is represented in the database. While access to the set of objects referenced by the attribute can easily be achieved by retrieving the set-valued attribute, the inverse operation is much more difficult (and costly). For example, a relationship between employees and departments may be recorded by creating a `Department` class which has an attribute 'hasEmployees' which holds the set of `Employee` objects who are members of a department. Then, the query to find the department of a given employee will require that each department object is retrieved in turn and the attribute 'hasEmployees' examined to see if the given employee is amongst the set of employee objects.

4.4.5   Terminology, notation, and syntax

Even within the three object-oriented databases that we have reviewed there is a wide variation in both the syntax of the languages and the terminology that is used. For example, in these systems there is a general correspondence between the terms 'class' and 'type', 'method' and 'function', 'message' and 'parameter', 'instance variable', 'property', and 'attribute', and so on. This variation is not only confusing to those who wish to make use of object-oriented databases, but it may also be a barrier to their acceptance into industry. As use and experience of object-oriented database systems grows, a common terminology may evolve. Note, however, that the 'seamless' approach, in which a programming language is extended with object-oriented database facilities, may prevent such a consensus emerging as each system will use the terminology of the underlying programming language.

4.5 SUMMARY

In this chapter a review of three object-oriented database systems has been provided in an attempt to reveal some of the characteristics of systems which are currently available. To provide a basis for comparison, an outline implementation of a simple example schema has been provided for each system. This has highlighted a number of important issues in the key area of data modelling within object-oriented databases. Some of these issues were examined in the discussion section which concluded the chapter.

The remainder of the comparison focused upon the system functions and implementation details of the example systems. In this area the object-oriented databases examined were found to be much less supportive. Where facilities for concurrency control and recovery were provided, they were in most cases implementations of traditional mechanisms (e.g. transaction locking). However, this seems to be the area in which object-oriented database systems are attempting to improve incrementally the mechanisms provided in database systems, in particular looking at new approaches to recovery, long-lived transactions, and object clustering.

5

OBJECT-ORIENTED DATABASE SUPPORT
FOR AN IPSE

Providing support for design applications has been one of the main driving forces in much of the work on object-oriented databases. Indeed, it has been claimed (Bernstein, 1987) that new approaches such as object-oriented databases are the only way to provide the necessary performance and functionality these applications require. Many people believe that simply attempting to augment a relational database with new facilities is inadequate.

While most of the work examining the use of object-oriented databases for design applications has concentrated on computer-aided design (CAD) of integrated circuits, or document retrieval and office information systems, database support for software design should also benefit from object-oriented technology. In particular, the central component of integrated project support environments (IPSEs) is a data repository which must exhibit many of the characteristics of equivalent storage managers for other design applications (Brown, 1989). In this section we examine the requirements for databases within an IPSE, show how object-oriented databases provide many of the necessary qualities, and briefly examine some IPSE systems which claim to be centred around an object-oriented database component.

5.1   WHY OBJECT-ORIENTED DATABASES FOR AN IPSE?

The data storage component of an IPSE, often referred to as an object management system (OMS), has been the subject of much research interest over the past few years. Following the recommendations of the Stoneman report (Buxton, 1980) for the architecture of an Ada programming support environment (APSE), the use of a database system as the central integrating component of support environments has been investigated. However, as we reviewed in Chapter 1, existing database technology does not satisfy many of the OMS requirements. It is useful to examine these requirements briefly and satisfy ourselves that an object-oriented database system, used as the OMS component of an IPSE, will more closely match the requirements than a traditional (relational) database system.[1]

5.1.1   OMS requirements

Many researchers have examined the necessary database requirements for the OMS component of an IPSE (Bernstein and Lomet, 1987; Brown, 1989; Read, 1989). For this brief look at object-oriented database systems, we make use of a set of high-level OMS requirements common to earlier work, and consistent with the outline database requirements identified in Chapter 1. For each requirement defined, we briefly state the requirement, and then discuss it with respect to how an object-oriented database system addresses that requirement. No justification for the choice of OMS requirements is provided here. That has been addressed in detail in the original references (Bernstein and Lomet, 1987; Brown, 1989; Read, 1989).

- *Ability to extend the set of data types supported.*

  Fundamental to the object-oriented model is the ability to extend the class hierarchy with new classes. In most object-oriented databases the data types are represented as classes within the class hierarchy and can be augmented with ease.

- *Facilities to model hierarchical structures conveniently.*

  Again, the sub/superclass relationships are fundamental in the object-oriented model. This explicitly records hierarchical relationships between objects.

- *Direct representation of the software process, in particular by encapsulating operators (behaviour) with the data.*

  Another important part of the object-oriented model is the encapsulation of operators with data to provide behavioural support. This can conveniently be used to model the software process.

- *Control of redundancy and sharing of data.*

  The object base of object-oriented databases exhibits all the characteristics of traditional databases. In particular, mechanisms for sharing and multi-user access are provided.

---

[1]This exercise has also been carried out for design applications in general, reaching the conclusion that an object-oriented approach to data management is essential to future engineering information systems (Heiler *et al.*, 1987).

- *Support for long-lived transactions.*

   This may not always be provided in object-oriented databases. In some systems, such as ONTOS, a nested transaction facility is available which alleviates the problem to some degree. However, a number of research prototypes are attempting to tackle the problem through more complex mechanisms (Moss, 1986; Garza and Kim, 1988), in particular through the use of multiple object versions.

- *Version control for multiple (and complex) objects.*

   Object-oriented database systems such as Iris and ONTOS do have built-in version mechanisms. But even without this, the ease with which the predefined class hierarchy can be expanded means that it is relatively easy to define your own version mechanism.

- *Consistency mechanisms to ensure the integrity of data.*

   While the modelling capabilities of object-oriented databases, particularly the behavioural modelling, help ensure database integrity, a number of systems are also experimenting with rule mechanisms, automatic triggering of procedures, and special facilities for recording derived data which is automatically kept up to date (Stonebraker, 1986; Hudson and King, 1986).

- *Recovery facilities for both hardware and software faults.*

   These are facilities which most database systems provide. Object-oriented database systems employ the same mechanisms as traditional database systems (transaction logging, checkpointing, and so on).

- *Distributed system support.*

   The importance of a distributed architecture has been recognized for many years, and most database manufacturers have released, or are currently working on, distributed versions of their products. The importance attached to this requirement is indicated by the fact that the first release of ONTOS will provide distributed host/client working over a homogeneous network of machines. Non-homogeneous distribution is promised for future releases.

- *Transparent distribution mechanisms.*

   Where object-oriented databases are providing support for distribution, the placement of data on different nodes, and its subsequent fetching, it is system managed and transparent to the user.

- *Adequate performance for design applications.*

   While performance has long been a concern of users of database systems, it is of particular concern to design engineers as design applications are typically large and complex. However, there are many researchers who believe that object-oriented database systems provide the best hope for supporting such applications (Bernstein and Lomet, 1987; Maier, 1986; Andrews *et al.*, 1989). Improving the performance of object-oriented database systems, through specialized object indexing mechanisms and new physical object clustering techniques, is an active area of research.

- *Security mechanisms to restrict access to sensitive data.*

  Security is an important issue in database systems. The object-oriented model provides direct support for restricting access to information through the encapsulation it enforces. A set of data is defined with the operators that are allowed to access it. This helps control the way the data is manipulated, and hides internal details which are not needed at the operation interface. In addition, a number of researchers are examining the use of the object model as the basis for defining different levels of security access (McDermid and Hocking, 1989).

- *Interfacing with existing and emerging standards.*

  For commercial viability, database manufacturers see the need to intercept, and anticipate, relevant standards. For example, where graphical tool interfaces are provided, as in Iris, the X Windows system is used. Similarly, ONTOS plans to add an SQL interface to its database system to allow existing tools and applications to be ported more easily.

5.2   REVIEW OF IPSES WHICH USE AN OBJECT-ORIENTED DATABASE

Due to the relative immaturity of the object-oriented database field, very few experiences of using object-oriented database systems can be found in the literature. In fact, while many papers discuss the issues in designing and implementing the database systems themselves, we are aware of only one generally available paper which describes the use of a commercially available object-oriented database system as the data repository for a set of design tools (Gupta *et al.*, 1989). In this section we look at the experiences described in this paper, and relate them to constructing a set of software design tools on a commercial object-oriented database. We then review an IPSE system which claims to use its own object-oriented data management facility for recording software engineering data. Finally, we briefly examine an influential research project which has produced an object-oriented database system specifically for use as the basis of a software development environment.

5.2.1 Use of a commercial object-oriented database system

CBase is the name given to a computer-aided VLSI circuit design system that has been developed at the University of Southern California (Gupta *et al.*, 1989). The basic design of CBase is a coupling of the VBase object-oriented database system to provide a data management facility, with the X11 window management toolkit to help develop a set of application tools with a graphical interface.

The CBase system was constructed to provide a common base for the many CAD application systems used at the University. Hence, it was important to provide a general, flexible framework for the computer-aided design of VLSI components. The second version of the CBase system, building on the experiences of the initial prototype, consists of a central core of type definitions which provide an initial schema for recording VLSI design data. On top of the schema definition, which includes the methods which access the data, is a set of tool interface routines. These are the basic interface operations which application programs use for displaying and interacting with the various VLSI design components. Finally, a general VLSI manipulation tool is provided to allow graphical user construction of VLSI designs through the schematic representation presented by the tool.

While the CBase designers discuss a number of minor disadvantages with the object-oriented approach to data management in general, and the VBase system in particular, their experiences appear very positive. The time taken to construct the system (the first version of CBase took two research students with no previous experience of object-oriented programming about seven months to build) and the ease with which the system could be refined and extended suggest that the approach has a number of clear attractions. In particular, with the relative immaturity of the field and the consequent need for experimentation, the CBase system provided a rapid prototype approach to support system design that was entirely appropriate. In this regard, they cite the following advantages of using an object-oriented data management approach:

- The object-oriented paradigm provides a powerful and flexible modelling approach for design applications. In particular, the object-oriented data model increases the ease with which complex entities can be directly represented owing to direct model support for generalization and specialization, object classification, and property aggregation.

- Increased reliability of the system owing to code reuse. As properties and methods are inherited from supertype to subtype, it is unnecessary to rewrite code. This helps to reduce the scope for introducing errors into the system.

- Operation definition and evaluation is simplified owing to the automatic method dispatch mechanism. For example, a request to invoke a method on an object may find a method specifically written for that object, or if not, will check each of the supertypes of that object to find an appropriate method to execute.

- The evolution of the type hierarchy must be expected in these applications. This is facilitated by allowing applications to access up-to-date meta-information, which is available in the same way as all user data. For example, the type hierarchy can be displayed to obtain the current set of types that have been defined.

- Exception handling typically takes up much of the coding effort in application programs. In an object-oriented approach exceptions are treated as objects. Thus, exception handling routines can be defined for general errors, and subsequently refined (within the type hierarchy) for more specific errors as the prototype evolves and new error modes are recognized.

Looking at the CBase work from an IPSE perspective, there seems to be a great deal that could be learned from using such an approach in a software design context. Indeed, there are a large number of interesting possibilities which a CBase approach could assist in investigating. These include the integration of existing tools into a design environment, evolution of the data schema and its effects on existing data instances, investigation of expected performance of such systems, the design and customization of user interfaces to a design environment, and many more.

5.2.2 Constructing a specific object-oriented data management facility

While it seems clear that in future IPSEs will want to make use of general-purpose object-oriented database systems, the current situation is that very few such systems are available in the marketplace. The result is that a number of IPSE systems have constructed their own data management facilities which exhibit many of the object-oriented database system characteristics. To illustrate the ways in which an object-oriented approach to data management is being used for supporting software design and development, we briefly look at the work being carried out at Atherton Technology in the USA.

The Atherton Tools Integration Service (ATIS) is a definition of an IPSE framework (Atherton Technology, 1988) produced by Atherton Technology. While the ATIS proposal is produced as a basis for discussion, Atherton Technology have produced, and market, a minimal implementation of the ATIS proposal under the name of the Software BackPlane (Passman, 1987).[1] One of the interesting aspects of the Atherton work is that the data management facilities began as a relational database, were extended to provide a more direct entity–relationship representation, and were finally replaced by an object-oriented system. The main motivation in this evolution was to simplify the interface to the data management facilities

---

[1] In fact, historically the ATIS proposal is a generalization of the Software BackPlane.

and provide better performance. In particular, it was found that the move from the relational to the object-oriented approach greatly reduced the number of data definition and manipulation operations that had to be defined and supported. This arose because of the inheritance mechanism which is employed in the type hierarchy. This encouraged properties and operators to be defined once, and inherited by subclasses where necessary. As a result, not only was the interface simplified, it also reduced the amount of code required to implement the operations through operation (method) reuse, and provided a more convenient and flexible mechanism for tool integration.

```
Element                    (invokes methods, keeps history, subtypes)
    NamedElement           (names and namespaces)
        Context            (for sharing and system modelling)
        User               (represents human user)
        Group              (represents any group of objects)
        Role               (working role for a user or group)
        Branch             (a set of logically related versions)
        Version            (an element that can be versioned)
            Type               (defines a type hierarchy)
                DataType       (represents a data type)
                ElementType    (describes this type hierarchy)
                PropertyType   (a classification of properties)
            Aggregation    (contains a set of objects)
                Collection     (a collection of references to versions)
                    MethodMap      (a "table" of methods available to a role)
                Text           (an element which permits text handling)
                    TextTool       (a script which represents a method)
                Binary         (an element representing binary data)
                    BinaryTool     (external code representing a method or tool)
            Tool           (a program that can be invoked)
            Method         (a function invoked in response to a message)
            Message        (a message with defined arguments)
    Relation               (undefined)
```

Figure 5.1   The predefined Software BackPlane type hierarchy

The minimal type hierarchy of the Software BackPlane is shown in Fig. 5.1. Indentation represents subtyping, and a short comment describing the type is given. The properties and methods which accompany each type are omitted for brevity.

```
Element                 (Type)
                        [subtype-of]
    Context             (History, Current-Directory, Toolset)
                        [change, invoke]
    Version             (Owner, Parent)
                        [checkout, checkin, status]
        Collection      (Children)
                        [attach, detach]
```

Figure 5.2   Details of the Software BackPlane type hierarchy

We obtain a useful illustration of the power provided through the use of the object-oriented approach to data management by considering the different ways in which an existing tool can be integrated into the Software BackPlane. A small part of the type hierarchy is examined in Fig. 5.2 with the properties of a type shown in round brackets, and the methods (operators) in square brackets. For example, if we wanted to integrate a dataflow diagramming tool into the Software BackPlane, we could achieve this by defining a new type with appropriate methods and adding this to the type hierarchy:

```
DataflowDiagram (ProcessScan, FlowScan, StoreScan)
                [open]
```

This new type would be defined as a subtype of Version. Hence, it would inherit the properties and methods of the Version type (and its subtypes). Tools can access the dataflow diagram tool's data by examining the properties ProcessScan, FlowScan, and StoreScan. Of course, tools which are written specifically to use the Software BackPlane would represent the data at a finer granularity for greater control and sharing.

Atherton Technology has been integrating tool sets on the Software BackPlane as customer requests have been received. Currently, at least the following tools are supported (to some extent) within the Software BackPlane: IDE's Software through Pictures, NASTEC Corporation's DesignAid from its CASE 2000 tool set, the UNIX tools such as cc, make, mail, grep, and troff, and the DEC VAXset products supporting Digital's Ada compiler.

5.3   AN OBJECT-ORIENTED DATABASE RESEARCH PROTOTYPE

While a number of research systems have been identified in previous chapters of this book, one particular system is worth describing in more detail as an example of the use of object-oriented database technology specifically for supporting software development activities. This is the DAMOKLES system, developed at the University of Karlsruhe in West Germany.

5.3.1   The DAMOKLES system

DAMOKLES is a prototype object-oriented database system which is aimed primarily at supporting large-scale software development (Dittrich *et al.*, 1987). The main component of the DAMOKLES system is its data model called the DAMOKLES object data model (DODM) which concentrates on supporting structured (or complex) objects which may exist in multiple versions.

The system is best illustrated with an example. Consider the DODM schema shown in Fig. 5.3, taken from a larger example in Dittrich *et al.*(1987). This shows the definition of a program object with name and author attributes, which is composed of a number of (versions of) subprogram objects. A subprogram object is defined to have a linear sequence of versions, and each subprogram can itself be composed of a set of subprogram versions.

The set of operators which are defined for DODM include facilities for allowing object instances to be created and destroyed, retrieval of object instances in sequential order according to type or via given attribute values, navigation within the subcomponents of a complex object, and copying of some part of, or all of a complex object.

Once coupled with facilities to define relationships between objects (either object types or object versions), DODM provides a powerful language for representing much of the information which typically exists in large-scale software development.

In addition to the DODM data model, the DAMOKLES project has experimented with a number of system functions which will be of benefit to software development applications. Notably, DAMOKLES includes support for multiple databases using an object as the unit of distribution, and long transactions using a check-in and check-out mechanism for shared data.

```
OBJECT TYPE program
  ATTRIBUTES
    name: STRING[30]
    author: STRING[20]
    ...
  STRUCTURE IS subprogram.version
END program


OBJECT TYPE subprogram
  ATTRIBUTES
    name: STRING[30]
    author: STRING[20]
    ...
  VERSIONS LINEAR
    ( ATTRIBUTES
        vers_name: STRING[30]
        vers_author: STRING[20]
        ...
    )
  STRUCTURE IS subprogram.VERSION
END subprogram
```

Figure 5.3   An example DODM schema

5.4   A FRAMEWORK FOR IPSE DEVELOPMENT

By examining a number of example object-oriented database systems and their application to software development support, we are now able to outline briefly a methodology for IPSE development based on these experiences. The steps which must be followed to develop an IPSE system based on an object-oriented database framework would typically be as follows:

1. Identify the (part of) the software development process which is to be supported in the IPSE. For example, we may decide that our IPSE should concentrate on supporting the path from requirements specification, through system design, to implementation in a programming language.

2. Define the objects which will be of interest in modelling this part of the development process. A starting point for this may be to decide which documents (requirements reports, specifications, code modules, etc.) are generated from

the process, and to trace their development through the software life-cycle. This should identify other important entities in the process such as resources, tools, and personnel.

3. Produce a model of the objects identified, and attempt to express the properties, operations, and relationships between the objects.

4. Extend the object-oriented database class hierarchy with the appropriate classes to represent the objects and their relationships. At this point a model of the software development process exists. This can be analysed to ensure it corresponds with the real-world situation. If not, the previous steps can be repeated.

5. Populate the database with instances of objects appropriate to the application being modelled. Information about a particular project is now represented (e.g. personnel, deadlines for producing documents, and so on). Also, the tools which will be used to support the development process can be integrated into the database. Ideally, the tools will be developed specifically for use with the object classes that have been defined, perhaps extending the class hierarchy as necessary. If foreign tools are to be integrated, a lower level of support may be provided (as described earlier for the Software BackPlane).

6. Finally, a high-level framework may be constructed around the environment to provide a more appropriate user interface for end users, customized to the work being carried out by the different kinds of IPSE end user.

5.5 SUMMARY

In this chapter we have reviewed one of the main application areas which has provided the driving force for much of the work in object-oriented database systems. In particular, we have examined a set of general IPSE OMS requirements with regard to the way in which object-oriented database technology may be seen as satisfying those requirements.

At present, experience of using object-oriented databases is rather limited, with few examples of the use of object-oriented database technology in the context of database support for software development. However, we have examined three particularly useful applications which reveal a number of interesting issues, and may point the way to the future of IPSE support using object-oriented databases.

The CBase system, coupling a graphical user interface with the VBase object-oriented database system, provided interesting feedback on the use of this technology in design applications (in this case VLSI design).

The Atherton Technology system, however, may be even more illuminating in that it shows a commercial IPSE product which has progressed from using a simple file store as the OMS component, through to an entity–relationship database, and has now moved into object-oriented database technology as providing the most promising way forward.

The DAMOKLES system sees control of object versions as a key issue in software development support, and focuses on this within its data model DODM.

It is clear that the application of object-oriented database systems to support software development will be an active area of research in the next few years. For example, the Arcadia project, a large collaborative research project in the USA, is examining various aspects of the problems of object management support for software development environments (Taylor *et al.*, 1989). As part of this work they have been using the VBase object-oriented database system as a prototyping vehicle for experimenting with a software development object management facility. Initial feedback from this work shows that the use of an object-oriented database has been crucial, providing a flexible, generic basis for experimentation (Penedo, 1989).

Indeed, object-oriented databases are now being viewed in industry as a viable approach to supporting design applications. This is backed up by a recent announcement that Index Technology, producers of one of the leading computer-assisted software engineering (CASE) tools, intends to use the ONTOS object-oriented database system as the data management component of all future releases of their CASE tool products.

In the next chapter, we conclude our introduction to object-oriented databases by summarizing the main points of the book, and looking to the future role of object-oriented database systems.

6

ANALYSIS AND CONCLUSIONS

In this book we have provided an introduction to object-oriented database systems, with particular emphasis on their role within an IPSE. While we have concentrated on identifying the main advantages provided by the object-oriented approach, in this final summary chapter we begin by noting that the cited advantages are balanced by corresponding limitations and drawbacks. The first section of this chapter outlines these limitations.

Following on from that discussion, we look forward to the possible role of object-oriented database technology in the near future. In particular, we identify the central position which object-oriented database systems may occupy as an integrating technology, supporting the overlap in the areas of software engineering, artificial intelligence, and database systems. The importance of object-oriented database systems to the work on IPSEs is also discussed in the context of future information system factories.

6.1   DISADVANTAGES OF THE OBJECT-ORIENTED APPROACH TO DATABASES

It is worth noting that there are a number of researchers who remain to be convinced that the work in object-oriented database systems is anything more than a peripheral issue. Indeed, some have gone as far as describing the work as 'misguided' (Laguna Beach Participants, 1989). While some of the reasons for their opposition have been touched upon in earlier chapters, it is useful to provide a summary of the cited disadvantages and limitations of the object-oriented approach to databases. The main points raised are as follows:

100

- *No formal semantics.*   A great attraction of the relational data model is that it has a sound mathematical basis; implementations of the relational model have been developed as manifestations of the underlying theory.

  In contrast, the object-oriented data model has developed in a much more *ad hoc* way, mainly through extensions to existing programming languages. There is no formal underpinning, with the consequence that great confusion exists in both terminology and functionality of object-oriented database systems. It is only as a response to the existing problems that attempts are now taking place to provide a common framework for understanding object-oriented database systems (Atkinson *et al.*, 1989), and to examine the formal basis of the object-oriented data model (Bancilhon, 1988).

- *Loss of relational simplicity.*   One of the attractions of relational database systems is that the model of data which is supported is sufficiently simple to allow end users to define their own database schemas, or to write simple queries, with the minimum of help and support from experienced database personnel. This effect is particularly apparent in relational systems based on the SQL language. Indeed, in some applications the simplicity of the relational language as a modelling notation has led to the database schema being used as a communication medium between systems analyst and customer, allowing the customer to help in the verification of the design before and during implementation.

  To a large extent the object-oriented model has compromised this simplicity in the hope of providing a greater modelling capability. Hence, the different representations of relationships, the more complex query languages, and so on, require a greater level of database expertise from the end user.

- *Navigational queries.*   The object-oriented model makes use of direct object references to represent relationships between objects. This has the consequence that access to data is essentially by navigating the object references (i.e. pointers) to move from one object to another. Limitations of the navigational approach to data as experienced in CODASYL systems (Manola, 1978) have been well documented, and some people see their reappearance as a retrograde step.

  In defence of navigational database access, some researchers actually believe that a navigational interface is required for many design applications which essentially consist of complex networks of relationships (Gallo *et al.*, 1986). However, forcing all database access to take this approach is bound to cause inefficiencies in many set-based operations.

- *No general query language.*   An important requirement of many design applications is support for general *ad hoc* queries. This is particularly evident in situations in which users browse a complex structure in some arbitrary way to discover how data items are related. Unfortunately, a large number of object-oriented database systems are specifically aimed at fixed interaction with complex structures; it is not at all easy to define *ad hoc* queries on the data. This behavioural rigidity, insisting that structures are only accessed through a fixed set of predefined methods, is in sharp conflict with both the experimental nature of schema design, and the continual evolution of a schema over time (Elmasri and Navathe, 1989).

- *Lack of support for dynamic processes.*   Object-oriented systems describe encapsulated data structures and operations. Hence, the behaviour of each object is predefined by the operations which have been written for that object. While this approach is entirely appropriate in many situations, it is not always a natural way to describe some dynamic (or active) process applications in which an object's behaviour changes dynamically throughout its lifetime.

6.2   FUTURE DIRECTIONS

By way of a summary, we look towards the future of object-oriented database systems, and the important role they may play in software engineering research and practice.

6.2.1   Integration of existing technologies

It is increasingly being found that large-scale software applications are required to record and query efficiently large amounts of data in the course of carrying out their tasks. Traditionally, all but a small number of business data processing applications have written special data-handling routines which have been optimized for the application being developed. They have not made use of existing database management system services for their data handling because of the storage space and performance penalties of employing large amounts of generalized database management software when most of the database services were not used in the application. However, as machines become more powerful with larger main memories, the attraction of using generalized database management systems is growing. Software engineers are beginning to realize that system development time is greatly reduced through using a database management system to provide data storage and querying facilities, a method of controlling concurrent access to shared data, and some measure of security and recovery services. Hence, this has led to increased use of database systems as components of image processing applications, knowledge-based systems, geographical information systems, real-time systems, and, of course, IPSEs.

All of these arguments point to the use of a database system as a central component of systems development (Elmasri and Navathe, 1989). This is illustrated in Fig. 6.1. In fact, it is the object-oriented database model which may be the key

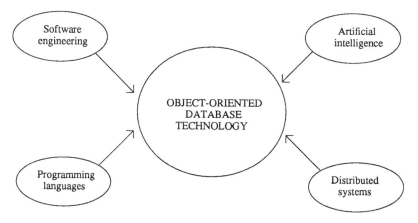

Figure 6.1   Information systems in the future?

to this integration as object-oriented database systems can be seen as embodying elements of:

- software engineering—through encouraging inheritance and reuse of class definitions both within a single application, and between applications;

- artificial intelligence—as deductive capabilities and logic-based approaches to object-oriented data models are developed, such as in the Generis system;

- programming languages—with many object-oriented databases developed as extensions to existing programming languages such as C++ and Smalltalk;

- distribution—the notion of an 'object' can be used as the basis of distribution as has been shown in distributed operating systems such as Clouds (Dasgupta et al., 1988).

6.2.2   An object-oriented approach to version control

One of the key areas of large-scale software development support concerns the identification, control, and manipulation of multiple versions of software components. A major cause of many costly software development errors is incorrect tracking of the large number of different versions of designs, test reports, specifications, software modules, and so on.

In future IPSE systems, the use of object-oriented techniques may help the tasks of version control and configuration management in two interesting ways:

1. An object-oriented database encourages the modularization of data into smaller components through the use of a specialization hierarchy. As a result, data is recorded at a finer granularity with the likelihood that a majority of the granules will remain largely unchanged. For example, if a program is recorded as a hierarchy of related modules, a change to one line of code in the program may only affect the module that contains that line, not the whole program. Hence, only a new version of that module is required. Typically, large sections of a program are never amended, and the possibility exists for improving system performance by taking advantage of this.

2. There are strong similarities between the organization of objects in an object-oriented database system and the version hierarchy which is maintained in a version control system. For example, we can think of a new version of a component as a specialization of its previous version. As such it inherits much of the behaviour of its parent object (i.e. it will respond to the same operations), but may have some additional behaviour. Viewing a version control system in this way may provide a more direct, and hence cleaner, approach to implementing such a system on top of an object-oriented database system.

This area is one clear example of how an object-oriented approach may be applied to different aspects of the software development process to provide a new insight. By building an IPSE directly on top of an object-oriented database, there is then a direct mapping to an implementation. Another area which may benefit in this way is software process modelling, where the use of an object-oriented approach to process modelling languages and techniques may well prove profitable.

6.2.3 The information systems factory

Many people believe that the future of integrated support for large-scale software development lies in the concept of *information systems factories (ISFs)* (Oddy and Tully, 1988). An ISF extends the notion of an IPSE in a number of important ways:

*   An ISF is aimed at supporting the development of the *complete* computer system, both hardware and software components.

*   Not only passive data storage support should be provided in an ISF, but also active support through the use of artificial intelligence and knowledge-based techniques.

- Support for a wide range of different development projects should be provided in an ISF through *open* system support. This implies that an ISF must be configurable to the many different styles of project management.

While the possibility of realizing the concepts of a true ISF may be some way off, the key to this ideal may be the work which is taking place in *software process modelling* (Tully, 1988). The aim of this work is to try to provide appropriate notations for describing the software development process which a development environment is designed to support. By understanding and representing the complex interactions which must take place, the process description forms the focal point for understanding the relationship between users, tools, management controls, and so on.

For example, one approach is to view the software development process as a set of interacting *activities*. Each activity will have a description which defines its resource requirements in terms of the information (documents, reports, test suites, and so on) and tools (editors, compilers, design tools, and so on) which may be used in its execution. Relationships between activities define the development process which must be followed as users are assigned and execute the activities. Of course, activities may be viewed hierarchically, as one activity may be executed by spawning many other subactivities which are delegated to other developers to be executed.

To be of use, this view of the software process must be automated. Many people see the use of object-oriented techniques, particularly object-oriented databases, as the ideal vehicle for doing this. The model of data as a set of interacting objects, maintained within a hierarchy (or graph) of object classes, maps very well on to the high-level view of interacting activities described above. This area of work is currently a very active area of research, and holds much hope for the realization of future ISFs.

6.3 SUMMARY

In this book we have provided an introduction to object-oriented databases with emphasis on their use as the data management component of an IPSE. Starting from first principles, the background to, and characteristics of, the object-oriented model have been discussed, leading to an analysis of the object-oriented concept as it is being applied to database systems. As can be expected with such a new technology, a wide variety of approaches are being tried. However, a number of common features are beginning to emerge, and these have been illustrated through reviewing the first object-oriented database products which have been produced and are now becoming more widely available.

While there is now general acceptance of the need for database technology to support large-scale software development, experience over the past few years has shown that the use of traditional (mainly relational) database systems for maintaining and manipulating design data has severe limitations. We have reviewed the data management requirements associated with IPSE systems, and shown the direct support that can be provided by using an object-oriented database to provide these services. To illustrate these ideas a number of systems which use an object-oriented data manager have been described.

The emergence of new approaches to database systems based on object-oriented principles can be seen as offering a new approach to IPSE system implementation. While many issues remain to be adequately addressed, the use of object-oriented databases within an IPSE should be seen as an important step in the direction of a truly *integrated* project support environment.

The pivotal role of object-oriented database technology, both in software engineering in general, and in IPSE systems in particular, will ensure that object-oriented databases will be an important research issue for a number of years to come.

REFERENCES

Agha, G. (1986), 'An Overview of Actor Languages', *ACM SIGPLAN Notices*, **21**(10): 58–67.

Andrews, T. and Harris, C. (1987), 'Combining Language and Database Advances in an Object-oriented Development Environment', in *Proceedings of the 2nd ACM Conference on Object-oriented Programming Systems, Languages and Applications*, pp. 430–440.

Andrews, T., Harris, C., and Sinkel, K. (1989), *The OB2 Object Database*, Technical Report, Ontologic Inc., Burlington, Mass.

Atherton Technology (1988), *Atherton Tools Integration Services (ATIS)— Phase 2 (ATIS01.03)*, Mountain View, Calif.

Atkinson, M.P. and Buneman, O.P. (1987), 'Type and Persistence in Database Programming Languages', *ACM Computing Surveys*, **19**(2): 105–190.

Atkinson, M.P., Chisholm, K., and Cockshott, P. (1981), *PS-Algol: an Algol with a Persistent Heap*, Technical Report, University of Edinburgh.

Atkinson, M.P., Morrison, R., and Pratten, G. (1987), 'PISA—a Persistent Information Space Architecture', *ICL Technical Journal*, **5**(3): 477–491.

Atkinson, M.P., Bancilhon, F., DeWitt, D.J., Dittrich, K.R., Maier, D., and Zdonik, S.B. (1989), 'The Object-oriented Database System Manifesto', in *Proceedings of the First International Conference on Deductive and Object-oriented Database Systems*, Kyoto, Japan.

Atkinson, M.P. (1978), 'Programming Languages and Databases', in *Proceedings of the 4th International Conference on Very Large Databases*, pp. 408–419.

Bancilhon, F. (1988), 'The Design and Implementation of O_2; an Object-oriented Database System', in *Advances in Object-oriented Database Systems*, Dittrich, K. R. (ed.), Lecture Notes in Computer Science, **334**, pp. 1–22, Springer-Verlag, Berlin.

Bate, G. (1986), 'MASCOT3 : An Informal Introductory Tutorial', *Software Engineering Journal*, **1**(3): 95–102.

Batory, D.S. and Buchmann, A.P. (1984), 'Molecular Objects, Abstract Data Types and Data Models—A Framework', in *Proceedings of the Tenth International Conference on VLDB*, Dayal, U., Schlateger, G., and Seng, Lim Huat (eds), Singapore.

Beech, D. (1988), 'A Foundation for Evolution from Relational to Object Databases', in *Advances in Database Technology—EDBT'88*, Lecture Notes in Computer Science, **303**, Springer-Verlag, Berlin.

Bernstein, P.A. and Lomet, D.B. (1987), 'CASE Requirements for Extensible Database Systems', *IEEE Database Engineering*, **10**(2): 2–9.

Bernstein, P.A. (1987), 'Database System Support for Software Engineering (An Extended Abstract)', in *Proceedings of the Ninth International Conference on Software Engineering*, pp. 166–177.

Bhateja, R. and Katz, R.H. (1987), 'VALKYRIE: A Validation Subsystem of a Version Server for Computer-aided Design', in *Proceedings of 24th ACM/IEEE Design Automation Conference*, pp. 321–327.

Bishop, J. (1986), *Data Abstraction in Programming Languages*, Addison-Wesley, Wokingham.

Booch, G. (1982), 'Object-oriented Design', *Ada Letters*, **1**(3): 64–76.

Booch, G. (1987), *Software Engineering with Ada (Second Edn)*, Benjamin/Cummings, Reading, Mass.

Bretl, R., Maier, D., Otis, A., Penney, J., Schuchardt, B., Stein, J., Williams, E.H., and Williams, M. (1989), 'The GemStone Data Management System', in *Object-oriented Concepts, Databases, and Applications*, Kim, W. and Lochovsky, F.H. (eds), pp. 283–308, Addison-Wesley, Reading, Mass.

Brodie, M. L., Mylopoulos, J., and Schmidt, J. W. (eds) (1984), *On Conceptual Modelling*, North Holland, Amsterdam.

Brooks, F.P. (1975), *The Mythical Man-Month*, Addison-Wesley, Reading, Mass.

Brown, A.W. (1988), 'The Relationship Between CAD and Software Development Support: A Database Perspective', *Computer-aided Engineering Journal*, **5**(6): 226–232.

Brown, A.W. (1989), *Database Support for Software Engineering*, Kogan Page, London.

Buchmann, A.P. (1984), 'Current Trends in CAD Databases', *Computer-aided Design*, **16**(3): 123–126.

Buxton, J.N. (1980), *Requirements for APSE—STONEMAN*, US Department of Defense.

Carey, M.K., DeWitt, D.J., Frank, D., Graefe, G., Muralikrishna, M., Richardson, J.E., and Shekita, E.J. (1986), 'The Architecture of the EXODUS Extensible DBMS', in *International Workshop on Object-oriented Database Systems*, Dittrich, K.R. and Dayal, U. (eds), pp. 52–65, IEEE Computer Society Press, New York.

Cheatham, T.E. (1981), 'Comparing Programming Support Environments', in *Software Engineering Environments*, Hunke, H. (ed.), North Holland, Amsterdam.

Chen, P.P. (1976), 'The Entity–Relationship Model—Toward a Unified View of Data', *ACM Transactions on Database Systems*, **1**(1): 9–36.

CISI-Ingenierie/MATRA (1986), *HOOD—Hierarchical Object-oriented Design (Issue 2.0)*, Paris.

Coad, P. and Yourdon, E. (1990), *Object-oriented Requirements Analysis*, Yourdon Press Computing Series, Yourdon Press, New York.

Codd, E. F. (1970), 'A Relational Model of Data for Large Shared Data Banks', *Communications of the ACM*, **13**(6): 377–387.

Codd, E.F. (1979), 'Extending the Database Relational Model to Capture More Meaning', *ACM Transactions on Database Systems*, **4**(4): 397–434.

Copeland, G. and Maier, D. (1984), 'Making Smalltalk a Database System', in *Proceedings of the ACM SIGMOD International Conference on the Management of Data*, pp. 316–325.

Dahl, O-J. and Nygaard, K. (1966), 'Simula—an Algol-based Simulation Language', *Communications of the ACM*, 9(9): 671–678.

Dahl, O-J. (1987), 'Object-oriented Specifications', in *Research Directions in Object-oriented Programming*, Shriver, B. and Wegner, P. (eds), pp. 561–576, MIT Press, Cambridge, Mass.

Dasgupta, P., Leblanc, R.J., and Appelbe, W.F. (1988), 'The Clouds Distributed Operating System', in *Proceedings of the 8th International Conference on Distributed Computing Systems*, pp. 2–9, San Jose.

Date, C.J. (1986), *An Introduction to Database Systems—Volume I*, Addison-Wesley, Reading, Mass.

Dittrich, K.R., Gotthard, W., and Lockemann, P.C. (1987), 'DAMOKLES—A Database System for Software Engineering Environments', in *Proceedings of the IFIP Workshop on Advanced Programming Environments*, Lecture Notes in Computer Science, **244**, Springer-Verlag, Berlin.

Dittrich, K.R. (1986), 'Object-oriented Database Systems: the Notion and the Issues (Extended Abstract)', in *International Workshop on Object-oriented Database Systems*, Dittrich, K.R. and Dayal, U. (eds), pp. 2–4, IEEE Computer Society Press, New York.

Downs, E., Clare, P., and Coe, I. (1988), *Structured Systems Analysis and Design Method: Application and Context*, Prentice-Hall, Hemel Hempstead.

Elmasri, R. and Navathe, S.B. (1989), *Fundamentals of Database Systems*, Benjamin/Cummings, Reading, Mass.

Feldman, S.I. (1979), 'Make—A Program for Maintaining Computer Programs', *SOFTWARE—Practice and Experience*, **9**: 255–265.

Fishman, D.H. (1989), 'An Overview of the Iris DBMS', in *Object-oriented Concepts, Databases, and Applications*, Kim, W. and Lochovsky, F.H. (eds), pp. 219–250, Addison-Wesley, Reading, Mass.

Gallo, F., Minot, R., and Thomas, I. (1986), 'The Object Management System of PCTE as a Software Engineering Database Management System', in *Proceedings of 2nd SIGSOFT/SIGPLAN Symposium on Practical Software Development Environments*, pp. 12–15.

Garza, J. F. and Kim, W. (1988), 'Transaction Management in an Object-oriented Database System', in *Proceedings of the ACM SIGMOD International Conference on the Management of Data*, pp. 37–45.

Glass, R.L. (1982), *Modern Programming Practices—A Report from Industry*, Prentice-Hall, Englewood Cliffs, N.J.

Goldberg, A. and Robson, D. (1983), *Smalltalk-80: The Language and its Implementation*, Addison-Wesley, Reading, Mass.

Graphael Inc. (1988), *G-Base version 3—Introductory Guide*, California.

Gupta, R., Cheng, W.H., Gupta, R., Hardonag, I., and Breuer, M. A. (1989), 'An Object-oriented VLSI CAD Framework', *IEEE Computer*, **22**(5): 28–37.

Heiler, S., Dayal, U., Orenstein, J., and Radke-Sproull, S. (1987), 'An Object-oriented Approach to Data Management: Why Design Databases Need It', in *Proceedings 24th ACM/IEEE Design Automation Conference*, pp. 335–340.

Hudson, S.E. and King, R. (1986), 'CACTIS: A Database System for Specifying Functionally Defined Data', in *International Workshop on Object-oriented Database Systems*, Dittrich, K.R. and Dayal, U. (eds), pp. 26–37, IEEE Computer Society Press, New York.

Huff, K. (1981), 'A Database Model for Effective Configuration Management in the Programming Environment', in *Proceedings of the 5th International Conference on Software Engineering*, pp. 54–61.

Hull, R. and King, R. (1987), 'Semantic Database Modelling: Survey, Applications, and Research Issues', *ACM Computing Surveys*, **19**(3): 201–260.

Jones, C.B. (1986), *Systematic Software Development using VDM*, Prentice-Hall, Hemel Hempstead.

Joseph, J., Thatte, S., Thompson, C., and Wells, D. (1989), 'Report on the Object-oriented Database Workshop', *ACM SIGPLAN Notices*, **24**(5): 31–51.

Katz, R.H. (1984), 'Transaction Management in the Design Environment', in *New Applications of Databases*, Garadin, G. and Gelenbe, E. (eds), Academic Press, New York.

Katz, R.H. (1986), 'Computer-aided Design Databases', in *New Applications of Databases*, Ariav, G. and Clifford, J. (eds), Academic Press, New York.

Kent, W. (1979), 'Limitations of Record-based Information Models', *ACM Transactions on Database Systems*, **4**(1): 107–131.

Kernighan, B.W. and Mashey, J.R. (1979), 'The UNIX Programming Environment', *SOFTWARE—Practice and Experience*, **9**(1): 1–16.

Kim, W., Banerjee, J., Chou, H.-T., Garza, J.F., and Woelk, D. (1987), 'Composite Object Support in an Object-oriented Database System ', in *Proceedings of the 2nd ACM Conference on Object-oriented Programming Systems, Languages and Applications*, pp. 118–125, Orlando, Florida.

Kim, W., Ballou, N., Chou, H.-T., Garza, J.K., and Woelk, D. (1989), 'Features of the Orion Object-oriented Database', in *Object-oriented Concepts, Databases, and Applications*, Kim, W. and Lochovsky, F.H. (eds), pp. 251–282, Addison-Wesley, Reading, Mass.

King, R. (1989), 'My Cat is Object-oriented', in *Object-oriented Concepts, Databases, and Applications*, Kim, W. and Lochovsky, F.H. (eds), pp. 23–30, Addison-Wesley, Reading, Mass.

Korth, Henry F. and Roth, Mark A. (1989), 'Query Languages for Nested Relational Databases', in *Nested Relations and Complex Objects in Databases*, S. Abiteboul, P. C. Fischer and Schek, H.-J. (eds), Lecture Notes in Computer Science, **361**, Springer-Verlag, Berlin.

Kuspert, K., Dadam, P., and Gunauer, J. (1987), 'Cooperative Object Buffer Management in the Advances Information Management Prototype', in *Proceedings of the 13th International Conference on Very Large Databases*, P. M. Stocker, W. Kent and Hammersley, P. (eds).

Laguna Beach Participants (1989), 'Future Directions in DBMS Research', *ACM SIGMOD Record*, **18**(1): 17–26.

Leblang, D.B. and Chase, R.P. (1984), 'Computer-aided Software Engineering in a Distributed Workstation Enviroment', *ACM SIGPLAN Notices*, **19**(5).

Lyngbaek, P. and Kent, W. (1986), 'A Data Modeling Methodology for the Design an Implementation of Information Systems', in *International Workshop on Object-oriented Database Systems*, Dittrich, K.R. and Dayal, U. (eds), pp. 6–17, IEEE Computer Society Press, New York.

Lyons, T.G.L. (1986), 'The Public Tool Interface in Software Engineering Environments', *Software Engineering Journal*, **1**(6): 254–258.

Maier, D. and Stein, J. (1987), 'Development and Implementation of an Object-oriented DBMS', in *Research Directions in Object-oriented Programming*, Shriver, B. and Wegner, P. (eds), pp. 355–392, MIT Press, Cambridge, Mass.

Maier, D. and Zdonik, S.B. (1990), *Readings in Object-oriented Database Systems*, Morgan Kaufmann, San Mateo, Calif.

Maier, D., Stein, J., Otis, A., and Purdy, A. (1986), 'Development of an Object-oriented DBMS', in *Proceedings of the Object-oriented Programming Systems and Languages Conference*, pp. 472–482.

Maier, D. (1986), 'Why Object-oriented Databases Can Succeed Where Others Have Failed', in *International Workshop on Object-oriented Database Systems*, Dittrich, K.R. and Dayal, U. (eds), p. 227, IEEE Computer Society Press, New York.

Manola, F. (1978), 'A Review of the 1978 CODASYL Database Specifications', in *Proceedings of the 4th International Conference on Very Large Databases*, West Berlin, IEEE.

McClure, C. (1989), *CASE is Software Automation*, Prentice-Hall, Englewood Cliffs, N.J.

McDermid, J.A. and Hocking, E.S. (1989), *Security Policies for Integrated Project Support Environments*, Technical Report (Unnumbered), University of York.

Meier, A. and Lorie, R.A. (1983), 'A Surrogate Concept for Engineering Databases', in *Proceedings of the 9th International Conference on Very Large Data Bases*, pp. 30–32.

Meyer, B. (1988), *Object-oriented Software Construction*, Prentice-Hall, Hemel Hempstead.

Morgan, H.L. (1986), 'Office Automation and Database Management', in *New Applications of Databases*, Ariav, G. and Clifford, J. (eds), Academic Press, New York.

Morgan, D. (1987), 'The Imminent IPSE', *Datamation*, **33**(7): 60–68.

Moss, J.E.B. (1986), 'Transaction Management for Object-oriented Systems', in *International Workshop on Object-oriented Database Systems*, Dittrich, K.R. and Dayal, U. (eds), p. 229, IEEE Computer Society Press, New York.

Moss, J.E.B. (1989), 'Object Orientation as a Catalyst for Language-Database Integration', in *Object-oriented Concepts, Databases, and Applications*, Kim, W. and Lochovsky, F.H. (eds), pp. 583–592, Addison-Wesley, Reading, Mass.

Mullery, G.P. (1979), 'CORE: Method for Controlled Requirements Expression', in *Proceedings of the 4th International Conference on Software Engineering*, New York, USA, IEEE.

Mylopoulos, J. and Wong, H.K.T. (1980), 'Some Features of the TAXIS data model', in *Proceedings of the 6th International Conference on Very Large Data Bases*, pp. 399–410.

Oddy, G.C. and Tully, C.J. (1988), *Information Systems Factory Study—Final Report (Volume I)*, Technical Report, UK Department of Trade and Industry.

Ontologic Inc. (1988), *VBase+ Functional Specification*, Burlington, Mass.

Ontologic Inc. (1989), *OB2 Client Library Reference*, Burlington, Mass.

Passman, W. (1987), 'Architecture of an Integration and Portability Platform', in *Proceedings of COMPCIN 32nd IEEE Computer Society International Conference*.

Penedo, M. (1989), 'Acquiring Experiences with Executable Process Models', in *Proceedings of the 5th International Software Process Workshop*.

Penney, D.J. and Stein, J. (1987), 'Class Modification in the GemStone Object-oriented DBMS', in *Proceedings of the 2nd ACM Conference on Object-oriented Programming Systems, Languages and Applications*, pp. 111–117, Orlando, Florida.

Read, N. (1989), *Object Management System—Present Requirements*, Technical Report ITC.RES.OMS-REQ, British Telecom Research Laboratories, Ipswich.

Rentsch, T. (1982), 'Object-oriented Programming', *ACM SIGPLAN Notices*, **17**(9): 51–57.

Rowe, L.A. and Shoens, K.A. (1979), 'Data Abstraction, Views and Updates in RIGEL', in *Proceedings of ACM SIGMOD'79*.

Rowland, B.R. and Welsch, R.J. (1983), 'Software Development System', *Bell Systems Technical Journal*, **62**(1): 275–289.

Schmidt, J.W. (1977), 'Some High-level Language Constructs for Data of Type Relation', *ACM TODS*, **2**(3): 247–261.

Servio Logic Corporation (1989), *GemStone—Product Overview*, Beaverton, Oregon.

Shaw, M. (1984), 'Abstraction Techniques in Modern Programming Languages', *IEEE Software*, pp. 10–26.

Skarra, A.H. and Zdonik, S.B. (1986), 'The Management of Changing Types in an Object-oriented Database', *ACM SIGPLAN Notices*, **21**(11): 483–495.

Skarra, A.H., Zdonik, S.B., and Reiss, S.P. (1986), 'An Object Server for an Object-oriented Database System', in *International Workshop on Object-oriented Database Systems*, Dittrich, K.R. and Dayal, U. (eds), pp. 196–204, IEEE Computer Society Press, New York.

Stonebraker, M. (1986), 'Object Management in POSTGRES Using Procedures', in *International Workshop on Object-oriented Database Systems*, Dittrich, K.R. and Dayal, U. (eds), pp. 66–72, IEEE Computer Society Press, New York.

Stonebraker, M. (1988), 'Future Trends in Database Systems', in *Proceedings of the Fourth International Conference on Data Engineering*, pp. 222–231, IEEE.

Sutcliffe, A. (1988), *Jackson Systems Development*, Prentice-Hall, Hemel Hempstead.

Taylor, R.N., Belz, F.C., Clarke, L.A., Osterweil, L., Selby, R.W., Wileden, J.C., Wolf, A.L., and Young, M. (1989), 'Foundations for the Arcadia Environment Architecture', *ACM SIGPLAN Notices*, **24**(2): 1–13.

Teitelbaum, T. and Reps, T. (1981), 'The Cornell Program Synthesiser: a Syntax-directed Programming Environment', *Communications of the ACM*, **24**(9): 563–573.

Tichy, W.F. (1982), 'Design, Implementation, and Evaluation of a Revision Control System', in *Proceedings of the 6th International Conference on Software Engineering*.

Tsichritzis, D. C. and Lochovsky, F. H. (1982), *Data Models*, Prentice-Hall, Englewood Cliffs, N.J.

Tully, C. (ed.) (1988), *Proceedings of the 4th International Software Process Workshop*, Devon, UK, ACM.

Ullman, J.D. (1988), *Principles of Database and Knowledge-base Systems— Volume I*, Computer Science Press, Rockville, Maryland.

Wasserman, A.I. (1979), 'The Data Management Facilities of PLAIN', in *Proceedings of the ACM SIGMOD International Conference on the Management of Data*.

Woodcock, J. and Loomes, M. (1988), *Software Engineering Mathematics*, Pitman, London.

Zhu, J. and Maier, D. (1988), 'Abstract Object in an Object-oriented Model', in *Proceedings of the 2nd International Conference on Expert Database Systems*.

Part II

An Annotated Bibliography

7

AN ANNOTATED BIBLIOGRAPHY ON OBJECT-ORIENTED DATABASES

This chapter provides an extensive bibliography of references to object-oriented database systems and their applications. As this is a relatively new area of research, there are no clear definitions available to help guide the scope of this bibliography. Hence, a wide interpretation of the term is used, based on the definition of object-oriented databases used by Dittrich [Dit86]. His informal definition of object-oriented database systems includes any database system which is based on a data model that allows each real-world entity, regardless of its complexity, to be represented by a single data model object. As a result, included in this bibliography are references which address:

- semantic data models and their implementations;

- nested and complex objects;

- general aspects of object-oriented programming;

- distributed systems which have a persistent object base.

As with any such undertaking, it is inevitable that many relevant papers and articles will have been omitted due to oversight or ignorance. All we can do is offer our apologies. Similarly, papers which have been published after the compilation of this bibliography will inevitably be omitted—*c'est la vie*. However, our main aim is to allow those interested in object-oriented databases, whether they are new to the area and require introductory material, or whether they are knowledgeable researchers interested in some detailed aspect of object-oriented systems, to be presented with pointers to the source material for future work.

7.1   ORGANIZATION OF THE BIBLIOGRAPHY

The main body of the bibliography consists of a long list of references sorted alphabetically on the surname of the primary author. While this ordering may be useful for identifying papers by a particular author, it is clearly of little help in many other situations. To try to remedy this a little, further sections provide lists of references which appertain to a series of broad categories.[1] Thus, some sort of guidance or limit is placed on searches for references relating to a particular subtopic or a particular system.

Within each category some of the references are accompanied by a short description of their content and by some brief editorial comments. These notes are provided to help guide the reader towards the relevant references. The presence or otherwise of a comment for a particular reference does not have any implication on the quality of that reference. However, in general the references which have been commented upon have been found to be particularly useful and informative.

The references are categorized as follows:

- *General concepts.*   These provide discussion on what it means for a database to be object-oriented. They are not specific to a particular system, but may specialize in some subtopic within the object-oriented domain. These references provide the starting place for those who know little about the concepts and characteristics of object-oriented databases.

- *Data model issues.*   The data modelling aspects of object-oriented databases are addressed in these references. They may be discussed in general terms, or with reference to a particular object-oriented data model.

- *Programming language and database integration.*   References in this category discuss the overlap between programming languages and databases, as well as extensions to programming languages to add a persistent object store, and also examine the similarities and differences between object-oriented programming languages and databases.

- *Comparisons between relational and object-oriented systems.*   As relational database systems are widely known, numerous references look at the limitations of these systems and define object-oriented databases by examining how they address those limitations. Other references use the relational model as the common base upon which object-oriented databases are defined.

---

[1]Note that the same reference may appear in several different categories if appropriate.

- *Complex objects.*   Support for the complex nature of objects is seen as a key issue in many application areas. These references examine the concept of support for complex objects. Areas addressed include the modelling of complex objects, query languages for hierarchical and recursive structures, and implementation issues for complex objects.

- *Persistent data stores.*   An important offshoot from the work on programming languages is the addition of persistent data types to conventional programming languages. These references directly address the issues involved.

- *Implementation details.*   Many references look at the practical issues in implementing an object-oriented database system. The references generally look at one aspect of the implementation of an object-oriented database, often in the context of a specific system.

- *Specific system descriptions.*   As more attention is directed towards the object-oriented database area, many people are attempting to build prototypes, or in a few cases production systems, which can be classed as object-oriented databases. These references describe specific systems. Some provide a broad overview of a complete system, while others look in more detail at some component of the system. The category is subdivided to group together references on some of the more well-known systems that have been developed. The systems treated in this way are:

  (a) GemStone
  (b) Iris
  (c) Orion
  (d) EXODUS
  (e) Cactis
  (f) POSTGRES
  (g) Genesis

- *Applications.*   There are a wide range of applications which object-oriented databases are said to support. Descriptions of the application of an object-oriented database to a particular problem domain are given in these references. Again, to help limit the search for references in a particular area, the applications are subdivided into the following application areas:

(a) engineering design

(b) computer-aided design of VLSI circuits

(c) software engineering

(d) expert and knowledge-based systems

(e) operating systems

(f) multimedia and office information systems

7.2 GENERAL CONCEPTS

[Dit86]

This paper provides a short overview of object-oriented database concepts. Following a brief examination of the main characteristics of an object-oriented system, a loose definition of object-oriented databases is proposed. This definition consists of three different categories of object-orientation for a database: *structurally object-oriented* databases provide support for representing complex data objects by a single database object; *operationally object-oriented* databases also allow the definition of (generic) operators which manipulate complex objects; *behaviourally object-oriented* databases allow the operators to be encapsulated in the structural definition of an object.

Finally, the paper notes that a number of important issues still require a great deal of further work (e.g. control of object versions, long-lived transactions, and support for large objects).

[ABD+89a]

A very useful introduction to object-oriented databases. The paper takes the form of a 'manifesto', attempting to provide a definition of object-oriented databases. The aim is to be contentious, and thus to encourage debate and discussion in this area.

The definition consists of a set of characteristics which a database system must possess to be called 'object-oriented'. These characteristics are divided into three categories:

1. *Mandatory.* These are support for complex objects, object identity, encapsulation, types or classes, inheritance, overriding and late binding, extensibility, computational completeness, persistence, secondary storage management, concurrency, recovery, and an *ad hoc* query language.

2. *Optional.* These include support for multiple inheritance, type checking and

inferencing, distribution, design transactions, and versions.

3. *Open.*   These unresolved issues can be addressed in different ways in each object-oriented database system. They include issues such as the programming paradigm supported, the representation system, the type system, and uniformity.

[MZ90]

An extensive collection of many of the most fundamental papers in object-oriented database systems research. While all the papers have been published elsewhere before, collecting them together provides an excellent reference book on this area. If you want one object-oriented database reference book for your shelf, this would be the one to have.

The 41 papers are divided into nine sections ranging from papers on fundamental object-oriented concepts, semantic data modelling, and implementation issues, through to user interface aspects, and design applications. Each section has a useful overview written by the editors, which draws out the main concepts being addressed in that section, and provides a brief overview of each of the papers.

As an introduction to the book, the editors also provide an extensive overview of the fundamental issues of object-oriented database systems, referencing the other papers in the book for further details on any of the issues raised.

[ZAKB+86]

An excellent introduction to object-oriented databases. Looks at the characteristics of object-oriented systems in general by examining the object-oriented approach as it is being applied in a number of different application areas, such as programming languages, databases, knowledge representation and AI, CAD systems, and office information systems. The paper then focuses on a number of significant problems which remain to be addressed, concentrating on issues such as performance. Then, the possibilities for database and programming language integration offered by the object-oriented model are discussed, followed by short sections on how constraints on data can be enforced in an object-oriented system. A very useful paper for anyone requiring an overview of the different application areas using an object-oriented approach.

[Mai86]

A brief discussion of the reasons why object-oriented databases may provide the way forward for design applications, particularly with regard to adequate performance. Having reviewed why relational database systems are often too slow for design applications, the paper gives a number of reasons for believing that object-oriented database systems can fetch and store data at the required rate. The reasons include: more direct data modelling of complex applications, the use of optimistic recovery techniques, and the use of direct object referencing reducing the overhead involved in frequent object de-referencing.

[H⁺87]

A very useful paper which discusses the advantages of the object-oriented database approach for design applications. First, the paper briefly examines the main charac-teristics of object-oriented systems. Then, the main data management requirements of design applications are reviewed, concentrating on the issues of persistence, op-erations and constraints as first-class objects, concurrency control and recovery, modelling of relationships, the ability to support derived views, and performance considerations. Finally, the object-oriented approach to data management is eval-uated against the data management requirements which have been defined.

The conclusion is that the object-oriented approach is indeed suited to design applications. In particular, the paper highlights five main areas of benefit: a model of data that is well matched to the designers' needs, a common framework for both low-level and high-level operations, support for engineering functions such as version control, encouragement of a modular approach to application development, and the availability of extensible, flexible, and tailorable services.

[KL89b]

A collection of 24 excellent papers which provide a snapshot of the state of the art at present. Papers by various authors, some previously published in journals, are divided into five categories: object-oriented concepts, object-oriented appli-cations, object-oriented database systems, architectural issues, and future research and development in object-oriented systems.

While there are many interesting papers, perhaps the most revealing are the later papers which look at future research issues, particularly a paper by Maier which looks at how database systems can be made fast enough to support design applica-tions.

[EN89]

A recently produced introductory database text. It is particularly interesting be-cause it not only covers basic database design and technology issues, but also has a very useful chapter on advanced semantic modelling concepts and their mapping to the relational model. Also included is a short (but useful) section on object-oriented database modelling, providing a useful summary of the advantages and disadvantages of this approach. In a later chapter on current database trends, new database applications such as office information systems and engineering systems are briefly examined.

In a section reviewing commercial database systems, a useful overview of the VBase system is provided as an example of an object-oriented database.

[Lag89]

This is a very interesting paper as it describes the discussions which took place when a group of very-well-respected database researchers were brought together to analyse possible future directions in database research. The group included Stonebraker, Rowe, Lockemann, Gray, Dayal, DeWitt, Maier, and Bernstein.

Object-oriented database systems was one area which seemed to have occupied an extensive amount of their time. The paper reports that all the participants had very strong but differing views on the importance of this work. They concluded that their confusion had a lot to do with widely differing understanding about what constituted an 'object-oriented database', and so they identified the need for a commonly understood definition as being of prime importance.

It seems that those in favour of object-oriented database research pointed to two main advantages of the approach: the extensibility and flexibility of the modelling approach, and the importance of inheritance as a way of helping to control the complexity of many applications. Those opposed to object-oriented database research claimed that the approach did not easily allow *ad hoc* querying of data to take place, and that it basically only supported navigational querying. In their view this seemed to be a return to the days of CODASYL.

[Ull89]

This is another recent database textbook. What makes it particularly interesting is that it concentrates on the more recent object-oriented concepts from the outset. For example, the opening chapter provides an overview of database systems, with object-oriented database systems and knowledge bases being seen as a natural extension of previous relational data modelling work. The chapter on data models looks at E–R modelling, semantic data modelling, and object-oriented data modelling.

A later chapter on object-oriented database languages takes the unique approach of treating CODASYL and IMS as early object-based languages, followed by a detailed review of the OPAL language, used in the GemStone object-oriented database system.

Other references

[ABD⁺89b, KS86a, KS86b, Tha87, Ste88, Pet87, KS86c, McL86, Mos86, Ban88a, BKK88, D⁺86, KC86, Ull87, Ull82, Sny87, Bat87, Kim88, Weg87, R⁺88, Ban88b, GV89, Nie89, Sto86a, Pas89, Str86a, ESS88, KV87, Mey88, Agh86, DN66, MER88, ME89]

7.3   DATA MODEL ISSUES

[Ken79]

One of the earliest (and clearest) examinations of the problems with relational and other record-oriented models. Kent argues that record-based models, while providing a simple and familiar representation for modelling data, suffer from a number of limitations. The main sections of the paper look at the use of record-based models to store the entities and relationships of a real-world application, and the problems of using symbolic values to name and identify entities.

Through the many examples used, one of the conclusions is that record-based models cannot adequately represent much of the required semantic information either accurately or unambiguously.

While the paper does not examine alternative models which solve many of these problems, it provides important background material for later work on semantic and object-oriented data models.

[HK87b]

A comprehensive examination of semantic data modelling constructs, followed by a survey of a number of semantic data models. The paper is divided into four main sections. The first section looks at some background concepts in semantic data modelling, relating the approaches taken to the current work in object-oriented programming and artificial intelligence. The second section provides a discussion of the main issues in semantic data modelling through an extensive tutorial example. A model called the generic semantic model (GSM) is defined for this tutorial, and issues such as abstraction, generalization, and aggregation are analysed in the context of GSM. The third section provides a survey of a number of semantic data models, classifying them with respect to their philosophical considerations, schema components, and dynamic components. The fourth section examines some implementation considerations, including user interfaces to semantic models, and the architecture of database systems based on semantic models.

[LK86]

This paper looks at a methodology for the design of information systems, with emphasis on using an object-oriented database as the supporting tool for that methodology. Following a brief description of the data model of the Iris object-oriented database, the paper continues by defining a design methodology for using the model. The methodology consists of the following steps:

1. Define appropriate object types for your application.

2. Define the relationship between the object types in a type hierarchy.

3. Define fundamental relationships between object types as predicate functions.

4. Define object properties as functions.

5. Define how the functions are to be implemented.

6. Define application-specific operations as new functions.

7. Define the encapsulation and protection mechanisms necessary for the application.

The paper then describes in some detail how this methodology can be applied to the Iris database system itself. Finally, some considerations for implementing this methodology are discussed.

[Ket86]

A short overview of ODM, an object-oriented data model for CAD applications. The main concepts embodied in ODM include: consistent support for both data and metadata, support for both active and passive data, extensive mechanisms for abstraction, an extensible set of operators, and the use of mechanisms for multi-stage design.

An interesting paper because it describes one of the earliest attempts at providing object-orientation in databases specifically for CAD applications.

[B+87]

A detailed description of some aspects of the data model of the Orion object-oriented database system. A brief overview of object-oriented concepts is provided, followed by a more detailed discussion of the issues which must be addressed in supporting a subtype graph. The Orion mechanisms for such support are then described.

The next sections deal with three important issues in object-oriented data models, namely control of schema evolution, composite object support, and maintenance of multiple object versions. For each of these issues the solution adopted by the

Orion database is described.

[Bro89c]

A discussion of object-oriented data models by considering them as an evolution from semantic data models. The main theme of the paper is that object-oriented database modelling techniques must be seen as a natural progression from semantic data models. The object-oriented models augment the structural aspects of the semantic data model with operational facilities, producing a more behavioural approach to data modelling.

The paper uses work in the Aspect project as an example. This project defined an extended version of Codd's extended relational model RM/T as its vehicle for supporting software development applications. The Aspect data model is seen as a bridge between semantic data models and object-oriented data models.

[Kin89]

The curious title of this paper is based on the fact that anything described as 'object-oriented' (even a cat!) becomes easier to sell in the marketplace.

However, the serious point of the paper is that semantic data models and object-oriented data models are different. The author summarizes the difference through describing the former as *structurally* oriented, while the latter are *behaviourally* oriented.

[Bee87]

An excellent discussion of the design of an object-oriented data model. To illustrate many of the fundamental concepts which must be considered in defining an object-oriented data model, an outline definition of a data model is provided using an abstract syntax.

The components of the model which are highlighted include object definition, object types and classes, object methods (or actions), assertions and constraints, and transactions. As an appendix to the paper an informal definition of the primitives of the model is given.

Other references

[KS86a, KS86b, MBH⁺86, KS86c, Osb86, Rao86, AH84, AH87a, C⁺82, HK86b, PM88, Hul87, Nij76, Shi81, TL82, Zdo86, BW85, Bor88, CDV88, CS88, JGF⁺88, JR88, Kim88, RS85, SZ86, Bee88b, SKL88, DD89, UD89, MCB89, CW85, NH86, Weg86, Wie86b, AD87, BB84, BK85c, BK85b, ZR88, McL88, HZ88a, DKT88,

Pet88, Fra88, Wil88, PG88, BGR88, KW88, GZ89, Lam89, KR89, Lin89, KFY89, SB89, B+89a, KL89a, HS89, AK89, HZ88b, SRHB89, BMS84, KC88]

7.4   PROGRAMMING LANGUAGE AND DATABASE INTEGRATION

[BZ87]

An excellent discussion of some of the issues involved in extending a programming language with a database system, or conversely, extending a database system with a complete programming language. Both of these lead to systems which are referred to as 'object-oriented databases'. While there appears to be consistency in the general direction of this work, the paper draws attention to the fact that there are major differences which are largely unresolved.

Following a brief review of the history and culture in which the programming and database work has been carried out, the paper tries to highlight the differences in approach and terminology between the programming language and database camps. To illustrate the problems, the paper focuses on the different approaches each has taken towards supporting triggers and constraints, query optimization, persistent data, classes and types, and large amounts of data.

The conclusion is that it can only be when these 'cultural' issues have been addressed that integration of database and programming language work will be effective.

[Mos89]

A very interesting paper describing the benefits of database and programming language integration. The paper discusses why the object-oriented paradigm appears to be the most sensible way to achieve this. The final section concludes with some of the research issues which remain to be solved before programming language and database integration can become a reality. These research areas include improving the performance of object-oriented systems, new transaction mechanisms to support cooperative working, and definition of new software development methodologies which are better suited to producing solutions which can easily be mapped on to object-oriented systems.

[Atk78]

One of the earliest, and most influential, papers which discusses the need for programming language and database integration. Analyses a number of possible approaches; extending a database with programming language constructs, adding programming language facilities to a database, and defining new persistent languages. The paper concentrates on the introduction of persistent data types into an existing programming language.

A very useful background paper.

[Kel86]

An informative description of the basis for unifying programming languages and databases. The object-oriented model is seen as possibly providing the key to this integration. The issues involved are discussed under the categories of composition, extensibility, lifetime, reference, atomicity, recovery, accessibility, sharing, correctness, and efficiency. A very readable paper.

[CM84]

This paper looks at some of the issues which must be addressed in adding a persistent object base to the Smalltalk language.

An initial section reviews the limitations of existing commercial database systems, identifying the main problems as being inextensible type definition facilities, artificial restrictions on legal database schemas, limited modelling power (particularly for complex design applications), and lack of support for historical data values.

These issues are then addressed in the context of the set theoretic data model (STDM) which forms the basis of the GemStone database system. Following a short overview of STDM, the paper discusses the way in which STDM and Smalltalk can be combined into a single system.

[RMS88]

This paper describes Alltalk, an object-oriented system developed by Kodak which attempts to integrate a persistent object store with the Smalltalk language.

The paper is particularly useful as it presents a very clear discussion of the issues involved in integrating a database system with an object-oriented programming language.

Other references

[Ste88, TKM86, Ber86, Nes86, Kee89, Str86b, AH87b, Ban86, Dat87, GR85, Kae86, K$^+$88, SB85, LS82, Lis82, DT88, LTP86, BHJ$^+$87, RC87, B$^+$88a, Ala89, Wha89, Gol81, TS82, MS88, SL88, SMR89]

7.5 COMPARISONS BETWEEN RELATIONAL AND OBJECT-ORIENTED SYSTEMS

[SZ87]

A very useful paper as it implements the same system (a multimedia document representation and retrieval system) using both a relational approach and an object-oriented approach. This seems to be one of the few papers which actually does a direct comparison of the two approaches by examining implementations in two representative systems. The paper concludes with a discussion of the advantages and disadvantages associated with each implementation. The Encore object-oriented database is the main vehicle used for implementation.

[Bee88a]

This paper describes a proposal for an object-oriented version of SQL, called Object-SQL (OSQL). The initial sections of the paper provide the rationale for wanting to evolve SQL: while it has many deficiencies, it is a widely used, well-understood language, and evolving from it may encourage the use of OSQL as an upwardly compatible way to use object-oriented techniques.

Following a detailed description of the syntax and semantics of OSQL, the example used throughout that description is then implemented in SQL. This is then directly compared to the OSQL implementation with the conclusion that the object-based model provides a more flexible solution to the problem.

[CR86]

A short, but very interesting discussion of the need to ensure that the many useful features of relational databases are not thrown away when developing an object-oriented database. In particular, the paper identifies the strengths of relational database systems as being support for multiple concurrent users, the ability to record large amounts of data, the provision of data independence, the use of a powerful *ad hoc* query language, and the availability of user interface support tools.

The approach recommended is to evolve from an existing relational system by adding object-oriented characteristics, rather than extending an object-oriented programming language with persistent classes.

[Cod79]

In this paper Codd defines an extended relational model called RM/T. This is an important paper because it introduces entity-level operations rather than tuple-level ones, and as it introduces the concept of independent entity identity through a surrogate concept. Later in the paper a mapping between the extended model and the relational model is also defined through the introduction of entity-relations (e-relations) and property-relations (p-relations), and by extending the data dictionary (or catalog).

The early sections of the paper provide a review of the criticisms of the relational data model, and RM/T is proposed as a way to address some of those criticisms through capturing more of the semantics in the data model. Hence, the paper provides important background to the object-oriented approach.

[DD88]

A very interesting paper as it seems to be one of the first attempts at benchmarking object-oriented databases. The authors attempt to use the Sun relational database benchmarks, comparing results for the VBase object-oriented database against the Ingres and Unify relational database systems. The paper describes how an application is written in the VBase system, and relates this to an equivalent relational design.

The results from the benchmark are quite favourable, showing that object-oriented databases can provide performance at least as good as relational systems.

The paper concludes by criticizing the benchmark itself, believing that to compare object-oriented databases a new benchmark will be required specifically aimed at object-oriented database systems. The main focus of the criticism is that object-oriented database systems are primarily aimed at design applications. Thus, the difference in characteristics mean that comparison using a simple commercial application is not a true test of the system's capabilities.

This is a good paper to look at when asked about relational versus object-oriented database performance.

Other references

[Bro89c, GV89, Kin89, Aha88, FMW88, Heu88]

7.6   COMPLEX OBJECTS

[SAS89]

A comprehensive collection of papers which discuss database support for complex objects. Most of the papers originate from a workshop on 'The theory and applications of nested relations and complex objects' held in West Germany in April 1987. Other papers have been added to broaden the scope of the book.

The papers cover various aspects of complex object support, divided into four sections: systems design, fundamental issues, database modelling, and database design.

[DPS86]

A review of a storage system for complex objects, describing in some detail the physical aspects of maintaining complex objects on disk. The paper begins with a description of a set of logical level operations which can be used for recording and manipulating complex objects. Then, the most detailed sections of the paper provide a comprehensive examination of the internal level requirements of a complex object storage manager.

A useful paper for anyone wanting to find out about how complex object models can be supported by an object storage manager.

[KBC+87]

A detailed description of the semantics of composite object support as implemented in the Orion object-oriented database system. A BNF definition of a composite object is provided as:

```
<composite object>  ::= <composite object root>
                                      <linked dependency>*
<linked dependency> ::= <instance variable> <dependent object>
<dependent object>  ::= <leaf object>
                     | <dependent object root> <linked dependency>*
                     | { <dependent object>* }
```

The paper continues by examining the effect on the composite object class hierarchy of changes to class definitions. A taxonomy of schema changes is described. Versions of composite objects are then discussed, and the design of the Orion version model is analysed.

Finally, some performance issues are highlighted. The Orion system makes use of composite objects to improve performance by using a composite object as the unit of physical database clustering, and as the unit of locking within transactions.

[KBG89]

This paper revisits the composite object concepts introduced in the paper above. Some problems with the original composite object model and its implementation are discussed: namely, restriction of composite objects to a strict hierarchy of exclusive component objects, insistence on a top-down development approach to the composite object hierarchy, and enforcement of cascading delete of component objects when a parent object in the hierarchy is removed.

The paper examines extensions to the composite object model to resolve these problems, and the implications of these extensions on schema evolution, versioning, and locking.

[PV86]

A very interesting discussion about the problems of implementing complex objects in a database. The paper reports on an analysis of a range of techniques for the storage of complex objects. The alternatives examined are the direct storage model (non-first normal form model), and various forms of normalized storage model.

The main difficulty in implementing a complex object model is said to be the conflicting goals of efficient support for retrieving a single complete complex object, with the retrieval of collections of related object subcomponents. Hence, there are trade-offs between clustering on full objects, or clustering on related object components.

Other references

[CK86b, BK85a, BK86, KCB87, KVC88, Zan85, BB84, BK85b, UD88, SL88, PD89, SAB+89, SS89, DG89, Hul89, ABGG89, Tak89, GZ89, Lam89, KR89, Lin89, KFY89, SB89, OY89, Spa89, Heu89, LL89, DK88, ESW88]

7.7   PERSISTENT DATA STORES

[AB87]

A comprehensive survey of programming languages with persistent data types. Examines the different approaches taken and reviews example systems.

An initial section provides a comparison between different approaches to persistent data stores by implementing a number of small examples in a programming language (Pascal), a relational data language, and a database programming language (Pascal/R).

The paper continues by reviewing other languages which incorporate a data model (e.g. DAPLEX, Taxis, and Galileo), then looks at the issue of polymorphism as it applies to database programming languages. Then, persistent languages are examined, including object-oriented database languages.

The paper concludes by describing a number of issues which can be seen from the review to require further development.

[AMP87]

A short overview of work currently being carried out by Atkinson and his colleagues. In the introduction to this paper, Atkinson notes that in many applications only 10 per cent of code is concerned with the application itself: the remainder is required to convert between database, programming language, and user interfaces. The PISA project is examining persistent programming languages as one way of attempting to reduce this.

Following an overview of some of the issues in persistent programming languages, the paper examines the relationship between persistent programming and the IPSE2.5 project. The IPSE2.5 project is investigating support for the development of large software systems, and the paper claims that persistent languages may provide an appropriate vehicle for their implementation.

Other references

[ABC+83, Low87a, Tha86, BA86, ML87, Wie86a, HB87, CAC+84, Low87b, DPSW89a, DPSW89b, HC88, MS88, M+88]

7.8   IMPLEMENTATION DETAILS

[KF88]

An excellent examination of a number of implementation techniques with regard to their effect on the performance of an object-oriented database. The authors identify four areas which they believe are particularly crucial to performance in object-oriented databases:

1.   storage structures for complex objects;
2.   query processing and execution strategies;
3.   techniques for recovery and concurrency control;
4.   efficient execution of language operators.

The paper concentrates on this last area, in particular, looking at the problems of performing equality operations between complex objects (both 'deep' and 'shallow' equality). The issues involved in the identification and removal of duplicate objects are also discussed. The implementation techniques considered are hashing, tagging, and inferencing.

[BLW88]

A very detailed account of the background to, and design of, the Genesis database system.

The semantic interface to Genesis is a functional data language based on DAPLEX and FQL. Following a detailed description of the Genesis data model (GDM), the paper provides a brief section on query optimization in the GDM. Then, the main sections of the paper provide a general introduction to the issues which must be addressed in implementing a functional data language, followed by a description of the way in which Genesis represents data items. Timings are given for three different implementation strategies: parse tree, data-driven, and demand-driven methods.

The final section examines some of the extensibility issues, indicating that functional data models allow the 'open-endedness' which is essential to future database systems. A simple graphics system is implemented in GDM as an illustrative example.

[MS86]

A detailed description of the indexing mechanism used in the implementation of the GemStone database system. The paper provides an overview of the role and importance of indexing in the GemStone system, followed by a detailed account of the design and implementation of the scheme that has been provided. The authors describe the results of initial performance testing, claiming that a 300-fold improvement is achieved by using an index to select one element from a collection of 10 000.

An excellent paper for someone who wants to read the details of how an object-oriented database system can store and retrieve objects efficiently.

[SZR86]

A discussion on the design and implementation of an object manager used as the basis for an object-oriented database. An initial section describes some of the issues which are important in a client/server architecture, and continues by looking at the transaction management mechanisms which have been implemented in the object server. These are based on single-level transactions in which a client copies objects from the server to the user's own workspace, returning them at the end of a transaction. For concurrency control, the system implements a two-phase locking protocol to provide serializable schedules, but allows non-serializable schedules through implementing a triggering mechanism. In this latter scheme, other users of an object are notified (via a trigger) when the object is updated by another user. A less rigorous form of deadlock detection is implemented to accompany this scheme.

Thus, on implementing an application the user chooses the concurrency scheme most appropriate for that application.

The GARDEN programming environment is described as an example of the use of this object server. This provides support for visual programming languages (i.e. languages which allow programs to be developed using a graphical interface) built on the object server that has been described.

[CK89]

A detailed discussion of different object clustering techniques and their effects on object-oriented database performance.

The paper analyses the typical object-oriented application access patterns by studying a group of VLSI CAD users who designed applications using an object-oriented data manager called OCT. The authors concentrate on the number of read operations versus the number of write operations (the read/write ratio) of the applications, and the density of the structures defined by those applications.

One of the main results of the paper is the definition of a run-time clustering algorithm which, under high structure density and large read/write ratio conditions, can improve system response by a factor of 200 per cent.

[Cle86]

A PhD thesis which describes the design and implementation of an object manager. Following a detailed description of its design, the paper continues with a look at its use in supporting a multimedia document display and retrieval application.

Other references

[Tha87, Tha86, Row86, DPS86, ADM86, But86, Lam86, Mai86, DHW88, BJRA85, C$^+$82, CK85, GD87, GW76, HZ87, KCB87, Sta84, PV86, KKD87, VD88, KKD89, VPF89, BKKK87, Har87, BMC88, DD88, C$^+$89a, K$^+$89b, PJF89, CF86, BD81, ZR88, KDG87, CL88, HK88a, B$^+$88c, KW88, Cat88, SC89, Thu89]

7.9   SPECIFIC SYSTEM DESCRIPTIONS

The GemStone system

[MS87, PS87, B$^+$89b, MS86, CM84, MSOP86, GM88]

The Iris system

[F$^+$87, Fis88, F$^+$89, LK86, Bee88a]

The Orion system

[K$^+$87, BKKK87, GK88, Kim88, WK87, K$^+$89a, BKK88, KCB87, K$^+$88, KKD87, KKD89, KBC$^+$87, KBG89]

The EXODUS system

[CDF$^+$86, CDRS86, C$^+$86, GD87, CD87, CDV88, RC87, CDV87, C$^+$89a, SC89]

The Cactis system

[HK86a, HK87a, HK88b, HK88a]

The POSTGRES system

[Sto86b, RS87, Sto87, SHH87, SR86, SAH87b, SAH87a, SR87, Row86]

The Genesis system

[Bat86, Bat87, BLW88, BBG$^+$88, MCB89]

Other references

[YI85, MD86, BCVG86, SCF$^+$86, AGOO86, OBS86, BM88, AEFEM86, DPS86, SZR86, ADM86, Ber86, But86, ZSGC86, DHW88, Kee89, Str86b, ABLN85, AH87b, BH86, Dat87, EE87, FO85, GM83, GR85, GD87, GW76, HZ87, Kae86, KV84, LRV88, Rot86, Shi81, TYI88, LS82, Lis82, DLA88, MT86, BR88, LTP86, SCB$^+$86, B$^+$88b, Osb88, Kor88, Zdo88, JK84, SO89, BHJ$^+$87, VD88, VPF89, ACO85, CS88, DVB89, GK88, GO87, Har87, JGF$^+$88, JR88, KLW87, MO86, MP87, OHK87, Osb87, RS85, WK87, SZ86, Cap87, SZ87, DGL87, B$^+$88a, CK88, WL88, Bro88, C$^+$89b, GCG$^+$89, Cle86, BMC88, Bro89b, Ath88, Kin86, W$^+$89, K$^+$89b, SZ89, DL85, GB84, SKL88, DD89, UD89, ZW85, HB87, LH89, LM88, CF83, KK88, CF86, Mas88, Low87b, DPSW89b, KDG87, F$^+$88, P$^+$88, HM88, Ber88, SSS88, DBM88, HC88, UD88, Aha88, FMW88, McL88, HZ88a, DKT88, Fra88, BGR88, KW88, MS88, SL88, O'B88, M$^+$88, HS88, AG89, OBBT89, B$^+$89a, SMR89, LSV89]

7.10 APPLICATIONS

Engineering design

[Eas86, Hae86, KH86, Rao86, BH86, DVB89, KLW87, KSW86, DL85, KK88, Ber88, H+87, CK88, HZ88b]

Computer-aided design of VLSI circuits

[BCVG86, Kat86, Ket86, Spo86, BKK85, CK86a, GB84, CF83, Afs85, BK85c, WL88, GCG+89]

Software engineering

[BL87, HK87a, Bro89b, Ath88, Hsi89, Str86a, PPT89, Bro88, Bro89a, Pet88, C+89b, DGL87]

Expert and knowledge-based systems

[YI85, DBM88, BD88]

Operating systems

[DLA88, MT86, B+88c]

Multimedia and office information systems

[AQ86, LH89, MO86, HS88, WKL86, SZ87, ABB+84]

BIBLIOGRAPHY

[AB87]   M.P. Atkinson and O.P. Buneman.
            'Type and Persistence in Database Programming Languages'.
            ACM Computing Surveys, **19**(2): 105–190, June 1987.

[ABB+84]   M. Ahlson, A. Bjornerstedt, A. Britts, S. Hulten, and L. Soderlund.
            'An Architecture for Object Management in OIS'.
            ACM Transactions on Office Information Systems, **2**(3): 173–196,
            July 1984.

[ABC+83]   M.P. Atkinson, P.J. Bailey, P. Cockshott, K.J. Chisholm, and R. Mor-
            rison.
            'An Approach to Persistent Programming'.
            Computer Journal, **26**(4): 360–365, 1983.

[ABD+89a]   Malcolm Atkinson, François Bancilhon, David DeWitt, Klaus Dit-
            trich, David Maier, and Stanley Zdonik.
            'The Object-oriented Database System Manifesto'.
            In *Proceedings of the First International Conference on Deductive
            and Object-oriented Database Systems*, Kyoto, Japan, December
            1989.

[ABD+89b]   M.P. Atkinson, F. Bancilhon, D. DeWitt, K. Dittrich, D. Maier, and
            S. Zdonik.
            'The Object-oriented Database System Manifesto'.
            Technical Report 30-89, Altair, France, August 1989.

[ABGG89]   Serge Abiteboul, Catriel Beeri, Marc Gyssens, and Dirk Van Gucht.
'An Introduction to the Completeness of Languages for Complex Objects and Nested Relations'.
In *Nested Relations and Complex Objects in Databases*, P.C. Fischer S. Abiteboul and H.-J. Schek (eds), Lecture Notes in Computer Science, **361**. Springer-Verlag, Berlin, 1989.

[ABLN85]   G. Almes, A. Black, E. Lazowska, and J. Noe.
'The Eden System: A Technical Review'.
IEEE Transactions on Software Engineering, **SE-11**(1): 43–58, January 1985.

[ACO85]   A. Albano, L. Cardelli, and R. Orsini.
'Galileo: A Strongly-Typed, Interactive Conceptual Language'.
ACM Transactions on Database Systems, **10**(2): 230–260, June 1985.

[AD87]   J. Annevelink and P. Dewilde.
'Object-oriented Data Management Based on Abstract Data Types'.
SOFTWARE—Practice and Experience, **17**(11): 757–781, November 1987.

[ADM86]   Malcolm P. Atkinson, Alan Dearle, and Ronald Morrison.
'A Strongly Typed Persistent Object Store'.
In *International Workshop on Object-oriented Database Systems*, Klaus Dittrich and Umeshwar Dayal (eds), p. 206. IEEE Computer Society Press, New York, September 1986.

[AEFEM86]   T. Lougenia Anderson, JR Earl F. Ecklund, and David Maier.
'Proteus: Objectifying the DBMS User Interface'.
In *International Workshop on Object-oriented Database Systems*, Klaus Dittrich and Umeshwar Dayal (eds), pp. 133–145. IEEE Computer Society Press, New York, September 1986.

[Afs85]   H. Afsarmanesh.
'An Extensible Object-oriented Approach to Databases for VLSI/CAD'.
In *Proceedings of the 11th International Conference on Very Large Databases*, pp. 13–24, 1985.

[AG89]   R. Agrawal and N.H. Gehani.
'ODE (Object Database and Environment): The Language and the Data Model'.

In *Proceedings of the 14th Annual ACM Conference on the Management of Data*, pp. 36–45, Portland, Oregon, June 1989.

[Agh86]   G. Agha.
'An Overview of Actor Languages'.
ACM SIGPLAN Notices, **21**(10): 58–67, October 1986.

[AGOO86]   A. Albano, G. Ghelli, M.E. Occhiuto, and R. Orsini.
'A Strongly Typed, Interactive Object-oriented Database Programming Language'.
In *International Workshop on Object-oriented Database Systems*, Klaus Dittrich and Umeshwar Dayal (eds), pp. 94–103. IEEE Computer Society Press, New York, September 1986.

[AH84]   S. Abiteboul and R. Hull.
'IFO: A Formal Semantic Database Model'.
In *Proceedings of the 3rd ACM SIGACT-SIGMOD Symposium on the Principles of Database Systems*, pp. 119–132, 1984.

[AH87a]   S. Abiteboul and R. Hull.
'IFO: A Formal Semantic Database Model'.
ACM Transactions on Database Systems, **12**(4): 525–565, December 1987.

[AH87b]   T. Andrews and C. Harris.
'Combining Language and Database Advances in an Object-oriented Development Environment'.
In *Proceedings of the Object-oriented Programming Systems and Languages Conference*, pp. 430–440, 1987.

[Aha88]   R. Ahad.
'The Object Shell: An Extensible System to Define an Object-oriented View of an Existing Database'.
In *Advances in Object-oriented Database Systems*, K.R. Dittrich (ed.), Lecture Notes in Computer Science, **334**, pp. 174–192. Springer-Verlag, Berlin, 1988.

[AK89]   S. Abiteboul and P.C. Kanellakis.
'Object Identity and a Query Language Primitive'.
In *Proceedings of the 14th Annual ACM Conference on the Management of Data*, pp. 159–172, Portland, Oregon, June 1989.

[Ala89]   S. Alagic.
Object-oriented Database Programming.
Springer-Verlag, Berlin, 1989.

[AMP87]   M.P. Atkinson, R. Morrison, and G. Pratten.
'PISA—a Persistent Information Space Architecture'.
ICL Technical Journal, 5(3): 477–491, May 1987.

[AQ86]   M. Adiba and N.B. Quang.
'Historical Multimedia Databases'.
In *Proceedings of the 12th International Conference on Very Large Databases*, pp. 63–70, Kyoto, June 1986.

[Ath88]   Atherton Technology.
Atherton Tools Integration Services (ATIS)—Phase 2 (ATIS01.03).
Mountain View, Calif., June 1988.

[Atk78]   M. Atkinson.
'Programming Languages and Databases'.
Technical Report CSR-26-78, University of Edinburgh, August 1978.

[B+87]   J. Banerjee *et al.*
'Data Model Issues for Object-oriented Applications'.
ACM Transactions on Office Information Systems, 5(1): 3–26, January 1987.

[B+88a]   N. Ballou *et al.*
'Coupling an Expert System Shell with an Object-oriented Database System'.
Journal of Object-oriented Programming (JOOP), pp. 12–21, June/July 1988.

[B+88b]   F. Bancilhon *et al.*
'The Design and Implementation of O_2, an Object-oriented Database System'.
In *Advances in Object-oriented Database Systems*, K.R. Dittrich (ed.), Lecture Notes in Computer Science, **334**, pp. 1–22. Springer-Verlag, Berlin, 1988.

[B+88c]   E. Bertino *et al.*
'The COMANDOS Integration System: An Object-oriented Approach to the Interconnection of Heterogeneous Applications'.
In *Advances in Object-oriented Database Systems*, K.R. Dittrich

(ed.), Lecture Notes in Computer Science, **334**, pp. 213–218.
Springer-Verlag, Berlin, 1988.

[B+89a]   A. Borgida *et al.*
'CLASSIC: A Structural Data Model for Objects'.
In *Proceedings of the 14th Annual ACM Conference on the Management of Data*, pp. 58–66, Portland, Oregon, June 1989.

[B+89b]   R. Bretl *et al.*
'The GemStone Data Management System'.
In *Object-oriented Concepts, Databases, and Applications*, W. Kim and F.H. Lochovsky (eds), pp. 283–308. Addison-Wesley, Reading, Mass., 1989.

[BA86]   P. Buneman and M. Atkinson.
'Inheritance and Persistence in Database Programming Languages'.
In *Proceedings of the 11th Annual ACM Conference on the Management of Data*, pp. 4–15, May 1986.

[Ban86]   F. Bancilhon.
'A Logic-programming/Object-oriented Cocktail'.
ACM SIGMOD Record, **15**(3): 11–21, September 1986.

[Ban88a]   F. Bancilhon.
'Object-oriented Database Systems'.
In *Proceedings of the 7th ACM SIGACT-SIGMOD Symposium on the Principles of Database Systems*, pp. 152–162, August 1988.

[Ban88b]   F. Bancilhon.
'Object-oriented Database Systems'.
In *Proceedings of the Joint ICL/University of Newcastle-upon-Tyne Seminar*. University of Newcastle-upon-Tyne, 6th-9th September 1988.

[Bat86]   D.S. Batory.
'Genesis: A Project to Develop an Extensible Database Management System'.
In *International Workshop on Object-oriented Database Systems*, Klaus Dittrich and Umeshwar Dayal (eds), pp. 207–208. IEEE Computer Society Press, New York, September 1986.

[Bat87]   D.S. Batory.
'Principles of Database Management System Extensibility'.
IEEE Database Engineering, **10**(2): 40–46, 1987.

[BB84]   D.S. Batory and A.P. Buchmann.
            'Molecular Objects, Abstract Data Types and Data Models—A
            Framework'.
            In *Proceedings of the 10th International Conference on Very Large
            Databases*, G. Schlateger U. Dayal and Lim Huat Seng (eds), Singa-
            pore, August 1984.

[BBG+88]   D.S. Batory, J.R. Barnett, J.F. Garza, K.P. Smith, K. Tsukuda, B.C.
            Twichell, and T.E. Wise.
            'Genesis: An Extensible Database Management'.
            IEEE Transactions on Software Engineering, **14**(11): 1711–1730,
            November 1988.

[BCVG86]   A.P. Buchmann, R.S. Carrera, and M.A. Vazques-Galindo.
            'A Generalized Constraint and Exception Handler for an Object-
            oriented CAD-DBMS'.
            In *International Workshop on Object-oriented Database Systems*,
            Klaus Dittrich and Umeshwar Dayal (eds), pp. 38–49. IEEE Com-
            puter Society Press, New York, September 1986.

[BD81]   A. James Baroody and David J. DeWitt.
            'An Object-oriented Approach to Database System Implementation'.
            ACM Transactions on Database Systems, **6**(4): 576–601, December
            1981.

[BD88]   P. Beynon-Davies.
            'Frames and Relations'.
            Computing Techniques, pp. 21–26, April 1988.

[Bee87]   D. Beech.
            'Groundwork for an Object Database Model'.
            In *Research Directions in Object-oriented Programming*, Bruce
            Shriver and Peter Wegner (eds), pp. 317–354. MIT Press, Cambridge,
            Mass., 1987.

[Bee88a]   D. Beech.
            'A Foundation for Evolution from Relational to Object Databases'.
            In *Advances in Database Technology—EDBT'88*, Lecture Notes in
            Computer Science, **303**. Springer-Verlag, Berlin, 1988.

[Bee88b]   D. Beech.
            'Intensional Concepts in an Object Database Model'.
            ACM SIGPLAN Notices, **23**(11): 164–175, November 1988.

[Ber86]   Arne-Juergen Berre.
            'Sharing of Objects in an Object-oriented Language'.
            In *International Workshop on Object-oriented Database Systems*,
            Klaus Dittrich and Umeshwar Dayal (eds), p. 209. IEEE Computer
            Society Press, New York, September 1986.

[Ber88]   A.J. Berre.
            'SOOM and Tornado-*: Experience with Database Support for
            Object-oriented Applications'.
            In *Advances in Object-oriented Database Systems*, K.R. Dittrich
            (ed.), Lecture Notes in Computer Science, **334**, pp. 104–109.
            Springer-Verlag, Berlin, 1988.

[BGR88]   K.V. BapaRao, A. Gafni, and G. Raeder.
            'The Design of Dynamo: A General Purpose Information Processing
            Model with a Time Dimension'.
            In *Advances in Object-oriented Database Systems*, K.R. Dittrich
            (ed.), Lecture Notes in Computer Science, **334**, pp. 286–291.
            Springer-Verlag, Berlin, 1988.

[BH86]   D. Bryce and R. Hull.
            'SNAP: A Graphics-based Schema Manager'.
            In *Proceedings of the 2nd International Conference on Data Engi-
            neering*, February 1986.

[BHJ+87]   A. Black, N. Hutchinson, E. Jul, H. Levy, and L. Carter.
            'Distribution and Abstract Types in Emerald'.
            IEEE Transactions on Software Engineering, **SE-13**(1): 65–76, Jan-
            uary 1987.

[BJRA85]   K. Birman, T. Joseph, T. Raeuchle, and A. El Abbadi.
            'Implementing Fault-tolerant Distributed Objects'.
            IEEE Transactions on Software Engineering, **SE-11**(6): 502–508,
            June 1985.

[BK85a]   F. Bancilhon and S. Khoshafian.
            'A Calculus for Complex Objects'.
            Technical Report DB-110-85, Microelectronics and Computer Tech-
            nology Corporation, Austin, Texas, 1985.

[BK85b]   D.S. Batory and Won Kim.
            'Modeling Concepts for VLSI CAD Objects'.
            ACM Transactions on Database Systems, **10**(3): 322–346, Septem-
            ber 1985.

[BK85c]   D.S. Batory and Won Kim.
           'Support for Versions of VLSI CAD Objects'.
           Technical Report, Dept of Computing Science, The University of
           Texas, Austin, Texas, September 1985.

[BK86]   F. Bancilhon and S. Khoshafian.
           'A Calculus for Complex Objects'.
           In *Proceedings of the 5th ACM SIGACT-SIGMOD Symposium on the
           Principles of Database Systems*, pp. 53–59, 1986.

[BKK85]   F. Bancilhon, W. Kim, and H. Korth.
           'A Model of CAD Transactions'.
           In *Proceedings of the 11th International Conference on Very Large
           Databases*, pp. 25–33, Stockholm, 1985.

[BKK88]   J. Banerjee, W. Kim, and K. Kim.
           'Queries in Object-oriented Databases'.
           In *Proceedings of the 4th International Conference on Data Engi-
           neering*, pp. 31–38, February 1988.

[BKKK87]   J. Banerjee, W. Kim, H.-J. Kim, and H.F. Korth.
           'Semantics and Implementation of Schema Evolution in Object-
           oriented Databases'.
           In *Proceedings of the 12th Annual ACM Conference on the Manage-
           ment of Data*, pp. 311–322, San Francisco, May 1987.

[BL87]   P.A. Bernstein and D.B. Lomet.
           'CASE Requirements for Extensible Database Systems'.
           IEEE Database Engineering, **10**(2): 2–9, June 1987.

[BLW88]   D.S. Batory, T.Y. Leung, and T.E. Wise.
           'Implementation Concepts for an Extensible Data Model and Data
           Language'.
           ACM Transactions on Database Systems, **13**(3): 231–262, Septem-
           ber 1988.

[BM88]   D. Beech and B. Mahbod.
           'Generalized Version Control in an Object-oriented Database'.
           In *Proceedings of the 4th International Conference on Data Engi-
           neering*, pp. 14–22. IEEE, February 1988.

[BMC88]   J.A. Brumfield, J.L. Miller, and H.-T. Chou.
           'Performance Modeling of Distributed Object-oriented Database
           Systems'.

In *Proceedings of the International Symposium on Databases in Parallel and Distributed Systems*, pp. 22–33. IEEE Computer Society Press, New York, December 1988.

[BMS84]   M. Brodie, J. Mylopolous, and J.W. Schmidt.
On Conceptual Modelling.
Springer-Verlag, Berlin, 1984.

[Bor88]   A. Borgida.
'Modeling Class Hierarchies with Contradictions'.
In *Proceedings of the 13th Annual ACM Conference on the Management of Data*, pp. 434–443, Chicago, Illinois, June 1988.

[BR88]   B.R. Badrinath and K. Ramamritham.
'Synchronizing Transactions on Objects'.
IEEE Transactions on Computers, **37**(5): 541–547, May 1988.

[Bro88]   A.W. Brown.
'An Object-based Interface to an IPSE Database'.
In *Proceedings of 6th British National Conference on Databases (BNCOD6)*, W.A. Gray (ed.), pp. 5–20. Cambridge University Press, Cambridge, 11th-13th July 1988.

[Bro89a]   A.W. Brown.
Database Support for Software Engineering.
Kogan Page, London, 1989.

[Bro89b]   A.W. Brown.
'Object-based Database Support for Software Engineering and the Aspect Project'.
In *Proceedings of the 1989 ACM SIGMOD Workshop on Software CAD Databases*, pp. 15–20, February 1989.

[Bro89c]   A.W. Brown.
'From Semantic Data Models to Object-orientation in Design Databases'.
Information and Software Technology, **31**(1): 39–46, January 1989.

[But86]   Margaret H. Butler.
'Storage Reclamation for Object-oriented Database Systems: A Summary of the Expected Costs'.
In *International Workshop on Object-oriented Database Systems*, Klaus Dittrich and Umeshwar Dayal (eds), pp. 210–211. IEEE Computer Society Press, New York, September 1986.

[BW85]   A. Borgida and K.E. Williamson.
            'Accommodating Exceptions in Databases, and Refining the Schema
            by Learning from them'.
            In *Proceedings of the 11th International Conference on Very Large
            Databases*, pp. 72–81, Stockholm, 1985.

[BZ87]   T. Bloom and S. B. Zdonik.
            'Issues in the Design of Object-oriented Database Programming Lan-
            guages'.
            In *Proceedings of the Object-oriented Programming Systems and
            Languages Conference*, pp. 441–451, October 1987.

[C⁺82]   A. Chan *et al.*
            'Storage and Access Structures to Support a Semantic Data Model'.
            In *Proceedings of the 8th International Conference on Very Large
            Databases*, pp. 122–130, September 1982.

[C⁺86]   M.J Carey *et al.*
            'The Architecture of the EXODUS Extensible DBMS: A Preliminary
            Report'.
            Technical Report 644, Computer Sciences Department, University of
            Wisconsin, May 1986.

[C⁺89a]   M.J. Carey *et al.*
            'Storage Management for Objects in EXODUS'.
            In *Object-oriented Concepts, Databases, and Applications*, W. Kim
            and F.H. Lochovsky (eds), pp. 341–370. Addison-Wesley, Reading,
            Mass., 1989.

[C⁺89b]   R. Conradi *et al.*
            'Design of the kernel EPOS Software Engineering Environment'.
            In *Proceedings of the International Conference on System Develop-
            ment Environments and Factories*, Berlin, May 1989.

[CAC⁺84]   W.P. Cockshot, M.P. Atkinson, K.J. Chisholm, P.J. Bailey, and
            R. Morrison.
            'Persistent Object Management System'.
            SOFTWARE—Practice and Experience, **14**(1): 49–71, January 1984.

[Cap87]   M. Caplinger.
            'An Information System Based on Distributed Objects'.
            ACM SIGPLAN Notices, **22**(11): 126–137, November 1987.

[Cat88]   R.G.G. Cattell.
           'Object-oriented DBMS Performance Measurement'.
           In *Advances in Object-oriented Database Systems*, K.R. Dittrich
           (ed.), Lecture Notes in Computer Science, **334**, pp. 364–367.
           Springer-Verlag, Berlin, 1988.

[CD87]   M.J. Carey and D.J. DeWitt.
           'An Overview of the EXODUS Project'.
           IEEE Database Engineering, **10**(2): 47–54, 6 1987.

[CDF⁺86]   Michael J. Carey, David J. DeWitt, Daniel Frank, Goetz Graefe,
           M. Muralikrishna, Joel E. Richardson, and Eugene J. Shekita.
           'The Architecture of the EXODUS Extensible DBMS'.
           In *International Workshop on Object-oriented Database Systems*,
           Klaus Dittrich and Umeshwar Dayal (eds), pp. 52–65. IEEE Com-
           puter Society Press, New York, September 1986.

[CDRS86]   M.J. Carey, D. DeWitt, J. Richardson, and E. Shetika.
           'Object and File Management in the EXODUS Extensible Database
           System'.
           In *Proceedings of the 12th International Conference on Very Large
           Databases*, pp. 91–100, Kyoto, August 1986.

[CDV87]   M.J. Carey, D.J. DeWitt, and S.L. Vandenberg.
           'A Data Model and Query Language for EXODUS'.
           Technical Report, University of Wisconsin-Madison, December
           1987.

[CDV88]   M.J. Carey, D.J. DeWitt, and S.L. Vandenberg.
           'A Data Model and Query Language for EXODUS'.
           In *Proceedings of the 13th Annual ACM Conference on the Manage-
           ment of Data*, pp. 413–423, Chicago, Illinois, June 1988.

[CF83]   L. Cholvy and J. Foisseau.
           'ROSALIE: A CAD Object-oriented and Rule-based System'.
           IFIP Congress, pp. 501–506, 1983.

[CF86]   Stavros Christodoulakis and Christos Faloutsos.
           'Design and Performance Considerations for an Optical Disk-based
           Multimedia Object Server'.
           IEEE Computer, **19**(12): 45–56, December 1986.

[CK85]   G.P. Copeland and S.N. Khoshafian.
           'A Decomposition Storage Model'.

In *Proceedings of the ACM SIGMOD International Conference on Management of Data*, pp. 268–279, May 1985.

[CK86a]   H.-T. Chou and W. Kim.
'A Unifying Framework for Version Control in a CAD Environment'.
In *Proceedings of the 12th International Conference on Very Large Databases*, pp. 336–344, Kyoto, August 1986.

[CK86b]   George P. Copeland and Setrag N. Khoshafian.
'Identity and Versions for Complex Objects'.
In *International Workshop on Object-oriented Database Systems*, Klaus Dittrich and Umeshwar Dayal (eds), p. 214. IEEE Computer Society Press, New York, September 1986.

[CK88]   H.-T. Chou and W. Kim.
'Versions and Change Notification in an Object-oriented Database'.
In *Proceedings 25th ACM/IEEE Design Automation Conference*, pp. 275–281, 1988.

[CK89]   E.E. Chang and R.H. Katz.
'Exploiting Inheritance and Structure Semantics for Effective Clustering and Buffering in an Object-oriented DBMS'.
In *Proceedings of the 14th Annual ACM Conference on the Management of Data*, pp. 348–356, Portland, Oregon, June 1989.

[CL88]   T. Connors and P. Lyngbaek.
'Providing Uniform Access to Heterogenous Information Bases'.
In *Advances in Object-oriented Database Systems*, K.R. Dittrich (ed.), Lecture Notes in Computer Science, **334**, pp. 162–173. Springer-Verlag, Berlin, 1988.

[Cle86]   G.M. Clemm.
'The Odin System: An Object Manager for Extensible Software Environments'.
Technical Report, University of Colorado, Boulder, 1986.

[CM84]   G.P. Copeland and D. Maier.
'Making Smalltalk a Database System'.
In *Proceedings of the ACM SIGMOD International Conference on Management of Data*, pp. 316–325, August 1984.

[Cod79]   E.F. Codd.
'Extending the Database Relational Model to Capture More Meaning'.

ACM Transactions on Database Systems, **4**(4): 397–434, December 1979.

[CR86]   R.G.G. Cattell and T.R. Rogers.
'Combining Object-oriented and Relational Models of Data'.
In *International Workshop on Object-oriented Database Systems*, Klaus Dittrich and Umeshwar Dayal (eds), pp. 212–213. IEEE Computer Society Press, New York, September 1986.

[CS88]   M. Caruso and E. Sciore.
'Meta-Functions and Contexts in an Object-oriented Database Language'.
In *Proceedings of the 13th Annual ACM Conference on the Management of Data*, pp. 56–65, Chicago, Illinois, June 1988.

[CW85]   Luca Cardelli and Peter Wegner.
'On Understanding Types, Data Abstraction, and Polymorphism'.
ACM Computing Surveys, **17**(4): 471–523, December 1985.

[D+86]   N.P. Derrett *et al.*
'An Object-oriented Approach to Data Management'.
In *Proceedings of COMPCIN 31st IEEE Computer Society International Conference*, pp. 330–335, March 1986.

[Dat87]   C.J. Date.
A Guide to the SQL Standard.
Addison-Wesley, Reading, Mass., June 1987.

[DBM88]   U. Dayal, A.P. Buchmann, and D.R. McCarthy.
'Rules are Objects too: A Knowledge model for an Active Object-oriented Database System'.
In *Advances in Object-oriented Database Systems*, K.R. Dittrich (ed.), Lecture Notes in Computer Science, **334**, pp. 129–143. Springer-Verlag, Berlin, 1988.

[DD88]   J. Duhl and C. Damon.
'A Performance Comparison of Object and Relational Databases Using the Sun Benchmark'.
ACM SIGPLAN Notices, **23**(11): 153–163, November 1988.

[DD89]   L.M.L. Delcambre and K.C. Davis.
'Automatic Validation of Object-oriented Database Structures'.
In *Proceedings of the 5th International Conference on Data Engineering*, pp. 2–9, February 1989.

[DG89]   Anand Deshpande and Dirk Van Gucht.
            'A Storage Structure for Nested Relational Databases'.
            In *Nested Relations and Complex Objects in Databases*, P.C. Fischer
            S. Abiteboul and H.-J. Schek (eds), Lecture Notes in Computer Sci-
            ence, **361**. Springer-Verlag, Berlin, 1989.

[DGL87]   K.R. Dittrich, W. Gotthard, and P.C. Lockemann.
            'DAMOKLES—A Database System for Software Engineering Envi-
            ronments'.
            In *Proceedings of IFIP Workshop on Advanced Programming Envi-
            ronments*, Lecture Notes in Computer Science, **244**. Springer-Verlag,
            Berlin, 1987.

[DHW88]   David L. Detlefs, Maurice P. Herlihy, and Jeanette M. Wing.
            'Inheritance of Synchronization and Recovery Properties in
            Avalon/C++'.
            Computer, **21**(12): 57–69, December 1988.

[Dit86]   Klaus R. Dittrich.
            'Object-oriented Database Systems: the Notion and the Issues (Ex-
            tended Abstract)'.
            In *International Workshop on Object-oriented Database Systems*,
            Klaus R. Dittrich and Umeshwar Dayal (eds), pp. 2–4. IEEE Com-
            puter Society Press, New York, September 1986.

[DK88]   M. Durr and A. Kemper.
            'Transaction Control Mechanism for the Object Cache of R2D2'.
            In *Proceedings of the 3rd International Conference on Data and
            Knowledge Bases*, pp. 81–89, Jerusalem, Israel, June 1988.

[DKT88]   H. Duchene, M. Kaul, and V. Turau.
            'Vodak Kernel Data model'.
            In *Advances in Object-oriented Database Systems*, K.R. Dittrich
            (ed.), Lecture Notes in Computer Science, **334**, pp. 242–261.
            Springer-Verlag, Berlin, 1988.

[DL85]   K.R. Dittrich and R.A. Lorie.
            'Object-oriented Database Concepts for Engineering Applications'.
            In *Proceedings of COMPINT '85: Computer Aided Technologies*, pp.
            321–325, September 1985.

[DLA88]   P. Dasgupta, R. LeBlanc, and W. Appelbe.
            'The Clouds Distributed Operating System'.

In *Proceedings of the 8th International Conference on Distributed Computing Systems*, pp. 2–17, June 1988.

[DN66]   O.J. Dahl and K. Nygaard.
'SIMULA—an ALGOL-based Simulation Language'.
Communications of the ACM, **9**(9): 671–678, September 1966.

[DPS86]   U. Deppisch, H.-B. Paul, and H.-J. Schek.
'A Storage System for Complex Objects'.
In *International Workshop on Object-oriented Database Systems*, Klaus Dittrich and Umeshwar Dayal (eds), pp. 183–195. IEEE Computer Society Press, New York, September 1986.

[DPSW89a] G.N. Dixon, G.D. Parrington, S.K. Shrivastava, and S.M. Wheater.
'The Treatment of Persistent Objects in Arjuna'.
The Computer Journal, **32**: 323–332, 1989.

[DPSW89b] G.N. Dixon, G.D. Parrington, S.K. Shrivastava, and S.M. Wheater.
'The Treatment of Persistent Objects in Arjuna'.
Technical Report 283, Computing Laboratory, University of Newcastle-upon-Tyne, June 1989.

[DT88]   S. Danforth and C. Tomlinson.
'Type Theories and Object-oriented Programming'.
ACM Computing Surveys, **20**(1): 29–72, March 1988.

[DVB89]   P. Dewan, A. Vikram, and B. Bhargava.
'Engineering the Object-relation Model in O-Raid'.
In *Proceedings of the 3rd International Conference, FODO '89*, pp. 389–403, Paris, France, June 1989. Springer-Verlag, Berlin.

[Eas86]   Charles M. Eastman.
'The Use of Object-oriented Databases to Model Engineering Systems'.
In *International Workshop on Object-oriented Database Systems*, Klaus Dittrich and Umeshwar Dayal (eds), pp. 215–216. IEEE Computer Society Press, New York, September 1986.

[EE87]   A. Ege and C.A. Ellis.
'Design and Implementation of GORDION, an Object Base Management System'.
In *Proceedings of the 3rd International Conference on Data Engineering*, pp. 226–234, May 1987.

[EN89]   R. Elmasri and S.B. Navathe.
            Fundamentals of Database Systems.
            Addison-Wesley, Reading, Mass., 1989.

[ESS88]   H.-D. Ehrich, A. Serndas, and C. Serndas.
            'Abstract Object Types for Databases'.
            In *Advances in Object-oriented Database Systems*, K.R. Dittrich
            (ed.), Lecture Notes in Computer Science, **334**, pp. 144–149.
            Springer-Verlag, Berlin, 1988.

[ESW88]   R. Erbe, N. Sudkamp, and G. Walch.
            'An Application Program Interface for a Complex Object Database'.
            In *Proceedings of the 3rd International Conference on Data and
            Knowledge Bases*, pp. 211–226, Jerusalem, Israel, June 1988.

[F⁺87]   D.H. Fishman *et al.*
            'Iris: An Object-oriented Database Management System'.
            ACM Transactions on Office Information Systems, **5**(1): 48–69, Jan-
            uary 1987.

[F⁺88]   S. Ford *et al.*
            'ZEITGEIST: Database Support for Object-oriented Programming'.
            In *Advances in Object-oriented Database Systems*, K.R. Dittrich
            (ed.), Lecture Notes in Computer Science, **334**, pp. 23–42. Springer-
            Verlag, Berlin, 1988.

[F⁺89]   D.H. Fishman *et al.*
            'An Overview of the Iris DBMS'.
            In *Object-oriented Concepts, Databases, and Applications*, W. Kim
            and F.H. Lochovsky (eds), pp. 219–250. Addison-Wesley, Reading,
            Mass., 1989.

[Fis88]   D.H. Fishman.
            'An Overview of the Iris Object-oriented DBMS'.
            In *Proceedings of COMPCIN 33rd IEEE Computer Society Interna-
            tional Conference*, pp. 177–180, March 1988.

[FMW88]   J.C. Freytag, R. Manthey, and M. Wallace.
            'Mapping Object-oriented Concepts into Relational Concepts by
            Meta Compilation in a Logic Programming Environment'.
            In *Advances in Object-oriented Database Systems*, K.R. Dittrich
            (ed.), Lecture Notes in Computer Science, **334**, pp. 204–208.
            Springer-Verlag, Berlin, 1988.

[FO85]   A.A. Farrag and M.T. Ozsu.
'A General Concurrency Control for Database Systems'.
In *AFIPS National Computer Conference Proceedings*, pp. 567–574, Chicago, 1985.

[Fra88]   A.U. Frank.
'Multiple Inheritance and Genericity for the Integration of a Database Management System in an Object-oriented Approach'.
In *Advances in Object-oriented Database Systems*, K.R. Dittrich (ed.), Lecture Notes in Computer Science, **334**, pp. 268–273. Springer-Verlag, Berlin, 1988.

[GB84]   J. Gerzso and A. Buchmann.
'TM—An Object-oriented Language for CAD and Required Database Capabilities'.
In *Proceedings of the IEEE Workshop on Languages for Automation*, pp. 115–123, 1984.

[GCG+89]   Rajiv Gupta, W.H. Cheng, Rajesh Gupta, I. Hardonag, and M.A. Breuer.
'An Object-oriented VLSI CAD Framework'.
IEEE Computer, **22**(5): 28–37, May 1989.

[GD87]   G. Graefe and D. DeWitt.
'The EXODUS Optimizer Generator'.
In *Proceedings of the ACM SIGMOD International Conference on Management of Data*, pp. 160–172, May 1987.

[GK88]   J.F. Garza and W. Kim.
'Transaction Management in an Object-oriented Database System'.
In *Proceedings of the 13th Annual ACM Conference on the Management of Data*, pp. 37–45, Chicago, Illinois, June 1988.

[GM83]   H. Garcia-Molina.
'Using Semantic Knowledge for Transaction Processing in a Distributed Database'.
ACM Transactions on Database Systems, **8**(2): 186–213, June 1983.

[GM88]   G. Graefe and D. Maier.
'Query Optimization in Object-oriented Database Systems: A Prospectus'.
In *Advances in Object-oriented Database Systems*, K.R. Dittrich (ed.), Lecture Notes in Computer Science, **334**, pp. 358–363. Springer-Verlag, Berlin, 1988.

[GO87]   D. Goldhirsh and J.A. Orenstein.
            'Extensibility in the PROBE Database System'.
            IEEE Database Engineering, **10**(2): 24–31, 6 1987.

[Gol81]   I. Goldstein.
            'Integrating a Network-structured Database Into an Object-oriented
            Programming Language'.
            ACM SIGPLAN Notices, **16**(1): 124–125, January 1981.

[GR85]   A. Goldberg and D. Robson.
            Smalltalk-80: The Language and its Implementation.
            Addison-Wesley, Reading, Mass., July 1985.

[GV89]   G. Gardarin and P. Valduriez.
            Relational Databases and Knowledge Bases.
            Addison-Wesley, Reading, Mass., 1989.

[GW76]   P. Griffiths and B. Wade.
            'An Authorization Mechanism for a Relational Database System'.
            ACM Transactions on Database Systems, **1**(3): 242–255, September
            1976.

[GZ89]   Ralf H. Guting and Roberto Zicari.
            'An Introduction to the Nested Sequences of Tuples Data Model and
            Algebra'.
            In *Nested Relations and Complex Objects in Databases*, P.C. Fischer
            S. Abiteboul and H.-J. Schek (eds), Lecture Notes in Computer Sci-
            ence, **361**. Springer-Verlag, Berlin, 1989.

[H⁺87]   S. Heiler *et al.*
            'An Object-oriented Approach to Data Management: Why Design
            Databases Need It'.
            In *Proceedings 24th ACM/IEEE Design Automation Conference*, pp.
            335–340, 1987.

[Hae86]   Theo Haerder.
            'New Approaches to Object Processing in Engineering Databases'.
            In *International Workshop on Object-oriented Database Systems*,
            Klaus Dittrich and Umeshwar Dayal (eds), p. 217. IEEE Computer
            Society Press, New York, September 1986.

[Har87]   M. Hardwick.
            'Why ROSE is Fast: Five Optimizations in the Design of an Exper-
            imental Database System for CAD/CAM Applications'.

In *Proceedings of the 12th Annual ACM Conference on the Management of Data*, pp. 292–298, San Francisco, California, May 1987.

[HB87]   David M. Harland and Bruno Beloff.
'OBJEKT: A Persistent Object Store With an Integrated Garbage Collector'.
ACM SIGPLAN Notices, **22**(4): 70–79, April 1987.

[HC88]   M. Hsu and T.E. Cheatham.
'Rule Execution in CPLEX: A Persistent Object Base'.
In *Advances in Object-oriented Database Systems*, K.R. Dittrich (ed.), Lecture Notes in Computer Science, **334**, pp. 150–155. Springer-Verlag, Berlin, 1988.

[Heu88]   A. Heuer.
'Foundations of Relational Object Management Systems'.
In *Advances in Object-oriented Database Systems*, K.R. Dittrich (ed.), Lecture Notes in Computer Science, **334**, pp. 209–212. Springer-Verlag, Berlin, 1988.

[Heu89]   Andreas Heuer.
'A Data Model for Complex Objects Based on a Semantic Database Model and Nested Relations'.
In *Nested Relations and Complex Objects in Databases*, P.C. Fischer S. Abiteboul and H.-J. Schek (eds), Lecture Notes in Computer Science, **361**. Springer-Verlag, Berlin, 1989.

[HK86a]   Scott E. Hudson and Roger King.
'CACTIS: A Database System for Specifying Functionally-Defined Data'.
In *International Workshop on Object-oriented Database Systems*, Klaus Dittrich and Umeshwar Dayal (eds), pp. 26–37. IEEE Computer Society Press, New York, September 1986.

[HK86b]   R. Hull and R. King.
'Semantic Database Modeling: Survey, Applications and Research Issues'.
Technical Report TR-86-201, University of Southern California, 1986.

[HK87a]   S.E. Hudson and R. King.
'Object-oriented Database Support for Software Environments'.
In *Proceedings of the 12th Annual ACM Conference on the Management of Data*, pp. 491–503, San Francisco, May 1987.

[HK87b]   R. Hull and R. King.
            'Semantic Database Modeling: Survey, Applications and Research
            Issues'.
            ACM Computing Surveys, **19**(3): 202–260, September 1987.

[HK88a]   S. Hudson and R. King.
            'An Adaptive Derived Data Manager for Distributed Databases'.
            In *Advances in Object-oriented Database Systems*, K.R. Dittrich
            (ed.), Lecture Notes in Computer Science, **334**, pp. 193–203.
            Springer-Verlag, Berlin, 1988.

[HK88b]   S.E. Hudson and R. King.
            'The Cactis Project: Database Support for Software Environments'.
            IEEE Transactions on Software Engineering, **14**(8): 709–719, June
            1988.

[HM88]   C. Hubel and B. Mitschang.
            'Object-orientation within the PRIMA-NDBS'.
            In *Advances in Object-oriented Database Systems*, K.R. Dittrich
            (ed.), Lecture Notes in Computer Science, **334**, pp. 98–103. Springer-
            Verlag, Berlin, 1988.

[HS88]   M. Hardwick and D.L. Spooner.
            'ROSE: An Object-oriented Database System for Interactive Com-
            puter Graphics Applications'.
            In *Advances in Object-oriented Database Systems*, K.R. Dittrich
            (ed.), Lecture Notes in Computer Science, **334**, pp. 340–345.
            Springer-Verlag, Berlin, 1988.

[HS89]   R. Hull and J. Su.
            'On Accessing Object-oriented Databases: Expressive Power, Com-
            plexity, and Restrictions'.
            In *Proceedings of the 14th Annual ACM Conference on the Manage-
            ment of Data*, pp. 147–158, Portland, Oregon, June 1989.

[Hsi89]   D. Hsieh.
            'Generic Computer-aided Software Engineering (CASE) Database
            Requirements'.
            In *Proceedings of the 5th International Conference on Data Engi-
            neering*, pp. 422–424, February 1989.

[Hul87]   R. Hull.
            'A Survey of Theoretical Research on Typed Complex Database Ob-
            jects'.

In *Databases*, J. Paredaens (ed.), pp. 193–256. Academic Press, New York, 1987.

[Hul89]   Richard Hull.
'Four Views of Complex Objects: A Sophisticate's Introduction'.
In *Nested Relations and Complex Objects in Databases*, P.C. Fischer S. Abiteboul and H.-J. Schek (eds), Lecture Notes in Computer Science, **361**. Springer-Verlag, Berlin, 1989.

[HZ87]   M.F. Hornick and S.B. Zdonik.
'A Shared, Segmented Memory System for an Object-oriented Database'.
ACM Transactions on Office Information Systems, **5**(1): 70–95, January 1987.

[HZ88a]   S. Heiler and S. Zdonik.
'Views, Data Abstraction and Inheritance in the FUGUE data model'.
In *Advances in Object-oriented Database Systems*, K.R. Dittrich (ed.), Lecture Notes in Computer Science, **334**, pp. 225–241. Springer-Verlag, Berlin, 1988.

[HZ88b]   S. Heiler and S.B. Zdonik.
'FUGUE: A Model for Engineering Information Systems and Other Baroque Applications'.
In *Proceedings of the 3rd International Conference on Data and Knowledge Bases*, pp. 195–210, Jerusalem, Israel, June 1988.

[JGF⁺88]   D. Jagannathan, R.L. Guck, B.L. Fritchman, J.P. Thompson, and D.M. Tolbert.
'SIM: A Database System Based on the Semantic Data Model'.
In *Proceedings of the 13th Annual ACM Conference on the Management of Data*, pp. 46–55, Chicago, Illinois, June 1988.

[JK84]   M. Jarke and J. Koch.
'Query Optimization in Database Systems'.
ACM Computing Surveys, **16**(2): 112–152, June 1984.

[JR88]   M. Jarke and T. Rose.
'Managing Knowledge about Information System Evolution'.
In *Proceedings of the 13th Annual ACM Conference on the Management of Data*, pp. 303–311, Chicago, Illinois, June 1988.

[K⁺87]   W. Kim *et al.*
'Features of the ORION Object-oriented Database System'.

Technical Report ACA-ST-308-87, Microelectronics and Computer Technology Corporation, Austin, Texas, September 1987.

[K⁺88]   W. Kim *et al.*
'Integrating an Object-oriented Programming System with a Database System'.
In *Proceedings of the Object-oriented Programming Systems and Languages Conference*, pp. 142–152, September 1988.

[K⁺89a]   W. Kim *et al.*
'Features of the ORION Object-oriented Database'.
In *Object-oriented Concepts, Databases, and Applications*, W. Kim and F.H. Lochovsky (eds), pp. 251–282. Addison-Wesley, Reading, Mass., 1989.

[K⁺89b]   W. Kim *et al.*
'Indexing Techniques for Object-oriented Databases'.
In *Object-oriented Concepts, Databases, and Applications*, W. Kim and F.H. Lochovsky (eds), pp. 371–394. Addison-Wesley, Reading, Mass., 1989.

[Kae86]   T. Kaehler.
'Virtual Memory on a Narrow Machine for an Object-oriented Language'.
In *Proceedings of the Object-oriented Programming Systems and Languages Conference*, pp. 87–106, September 1986.

[Kat86]   Randy H. Katz.
'Inheritance Semantics for Computer-aided Design Databases'.
In *International Workshop on Object-oriented Database Systems*, Klaus Dittrich and Umeshwar Dayal (eds), pp. 219–220. IEEE Computer Society Press, New York, September 1986.

[KBC⁺87]   W. Kim, J. Banerjee, H.-T. Chou, J.F. Garza, and D. Woelk.
'Composite Object Support in an Object-oriented Database System'.
In *Proceedings of the 2nd ACM Conference on Object-oriented Programming Systems, Languages and Applications*, pp. 118–125, Orlando, Florida, October 1987.

[KBG89]   W. Kim, E. Bertino, and J.F. Garza.
'Composite Objects Revisited'.
In *Proceedings of the 14th Annual ACM Conference on the Management of Data*, pp. 337–347, Portland, Oregon, June 1989.

[KC86]   S.N. Khoshafian and G.P. Copeland.
            'Object Identity'.
            In *Proceedings of the Object-oriented Programming Systems and Languages Conference*, pp. 406–416, September 1986.

[KC88]   W. Kim and H.-T. Chou.
            'Versions of Schema for Object-oriented Databases'.
            In *Proceedings of the 14th International Conference on Very Large Databases*, pp. 148–159, Los Angeles, August 1988.

[KCB87]   W. Kim, H. Chan, and J. Banerjee.
            'Operations and Implementation of Complex Objects'.
            In *Proceedings of the 3rd International Conference on Data Engineering*, pp. 626–633, May 1987.

[KDG87]   K. Kuspert, P. Dadam, and J. Gunauer.
            'Cooperative Object Buffer Management in the Advanced Information Management Prototype'.
            In *Proceedings of the 13th International Conference on Very Large Databases*, P.M. Stocker, W. Kent, and P. Hammersley (eds), September 1987.

[Kee89]   Sonya E. Keene.
            Object-oriented Programming in Common Lisp—A Programmer's Guide to CLOS.
            Addison-Wesley, Reading, Mass., 1989.

[Kel86]   Arthur M. Keller.
            'Unifying Database and Programming Language Concepts Using the Object Model'.
            In *International Workshop on Object-oriented Database Systems*, Klaus Dittrich and Umeshwar Dayal (eds), pp. 221–222. IEEE Computer Society Press, New York, September 1986.

[Ken79]   W. Kent.
            'Limitations of Record-based Information Models'.
            ACM Transactions on Database Systems, 4(1): 107–131, March 1979.

[Ket86]   Mohammad A. Ketabchi.
            'Object-oriented Data Models and Management of CAD Databases'.
            In *International Workshop on Object-oriented Database Systems*, Klaus Dittrich and Umeshwar Dayal (eds), pp. 223–224. IEEE Computer Society Press, New York, September 1986.

[KF88]   S. Khoshafian and D. Frank.
           'Implementation Techniques for Object-oriented Databases'.
           In *Advances in Object-oriented Database Systems*, K.R. Dittrich
           (ed.), Lecture Notes in Computer Science, **334**, pp. 60–79. Springer-
           Verlag, Berlin, 1988.

[KFY89]   Yahiko Kambayashi, Tetsuya Furukawa, and Hideki Yamamoto.
           'Realization of Nested Relation Interfaces for Relational and Net-
           work Databases'.
           In *Nested Relations and Complex Objects in Databases*, P.C. Fischer
           S. Abiteboul and H.-J. Schek (eds), Lecture Notes in Computer Sci-
           ence, **361**. Springer-Verlag, Berlin, 1989.

[KH86]   P. Kachhwaha and R. Hogan.
           'An Object-oriented Data Model for the Research Laboratory'.
           In *International Workshop on Object-oriented Database Systems*,
           Klaus Dittrich and Umeshwar Dayal (eds), p. 218. IEEE Computer
           Society Press, New York, September 1986.

[Kim88]   H.J. Kim.
           Issues in Object-oriented Databases Schemas.
           PhD thesis, University of Texas, Austin, May 1988.

[Kin86]   R. King.
           'A Database Management System Based on an Object-oriented
           Model'.
           In *Expert Database Systems*, L. Kerschberg (ed.), pp. 443–468. Ben-
           jamin/Cummings, Reading, Mass., 1986.

[Kin89]   R. King.
           'My Cat is Object-oriented'.
           In *Object-oriented Concepts, Databases, and Applications*, W. Kim
           and F.H. Lochovsky (eds), pp. 23–30. Addison-Wesley, Reading,
           Mass., 1989.

[KK88]   H.-J. Kim and H.F. Korth.
           'Schema Versions and DAG Rearrangement Views in Object-
           oriented Databases'.
           Technical Report, Dept of Computing Science, The University of
           Texas, Austin, Texas, February 1988.

[KKD87]   W. Kim, K. Kim, and A. Dale.
           'Indexing Techniques for Object-oriented Databases'.

Technical Report DB-134-87, Microelectronics and Computer Technology Corporation, 1987.

[KKD89]   K. Kim, W. Kim, and A. Dale.
'Cyclic Query Processing in Object-oriented Databases'.
In *Proceedings of the 5th International Conference on Data Engineering*, pp. 564–571, 1989.

[KL89a]   M. Kifer and G. Lausen.
'F-Logic: A Higher Order Language for Reasoning about Objects, Inheritance and Scheme'.
In *Proceedings of the 14th Annual ACM Conference on the Management of Data*, pp. 134–146, Portland, Oregon, June 1989.

[KL89b]   W. Kim and F. Lochovsky.
Object-oriented Concepts, Databases, and Applications.
Addison-Wesley, Reading, Mass., 1989.

[KLW87]   A. Kemper, P.C. Lockemann, and M. Wallrath.
'An Object-oriented Database System For Engineering Applications'.
In *Proceedings of the 12th Annual ACM Conference on the Management of Data*, pp. 299–310, 1987.

[Kor88]   H.F. Korth.
'Optimization of Object-retrieval Queries'.
In *Advances in Object-oriented Database Systems*, K.R. Dittrich (ed.), Lecture Notes in Computer Science, **334**, pp. 352–357. Springer-Verlag, Berlin, 1988.

[KR89]   Henry F. Korth and Mark A. Roth.
'Query Languages for Nested Relational Databases'.
In *Nested Relations and Complex Objects in Databases*, P.C. Fischer S. Abiteboul and H.-J. Schek (eds), Lecture Notes in Computer Science, **361**. Springer-Verlag, Berlin, 1989.

[KS86a]   M.L. Kersten and F.H. Schippers.
'A General Object-centered Database Language'.
Technical Report CS-R8615, Centrum voor Wiskunde en Informatica, 1986.

[KS86b]   M.L. Kersten and F.H. Schippers.
'Towards an Object-centered Database Language'.

Technical Report CS-R8630, Centrum voor Wiskunde en Informatica, 1986.

[KS86c]   M.L. Kersten and F.H. Schippers.
'Towards an Object-centered Database Language'.
In *Proceedings of the International Workshop on Object-oriented Database Systems*, Klaus Dittrich and Umeshwar Dayal (eds), pp. 104–112. IEEE Computer Society Press, New York, September 1986.

[KSW86]   P. Klahold, G. Schlageter, and W. Wilkes.
'A General Model for Version Management in Databases'.
In *Proceedings of the 12th International Conference on Very Large Databases*, pp. 319–327, Kyoto, August 1986.

[KV84]   G. Kuper and M. Vardi.
'A New Approach to Database Logic'.
In *Proceedings of the 3rd ACM SIGACT-SIGMOD Symposium on the Principles of Database Systems*, pp. 86–96, 1984.

[KV87]   S. Khoshafian and P. Valduriez.
'Sharing, Persistence, and Object-orientation: A Database Perspective'.
Technical Report DB-106-87, Microcomputer Corporation Technical Memorandum, Austin, Texas, April 1987.

[KVC88]   S. Khoshafian, P. Valduriez, and G. Copeland.
'Parallel Query Processing for Complex Objects'.
In *Proceedings of the 4th International Conference on Data Engineering*, pp. 202–209, February 1988.

[KW88]   A. Kemper and M. Wallrath.
'A Uniform Concept for Storing and Manipulating Engineering Objects'.
In *Advances in Object-oriented Database Systems*, K.R. Dittrich (ed.), Lecture Notes in Computer Science, **334**, pp. 292–297. Springer-Verlag, Berlin, 1988.

[Lag89]   Laguna Beach Participants.
'Future Directions in DBMS Research'.
ACM SIGMOD Record, 18(1): 17–26, March 1989.

[Lam86]   Winfried Lamersdorf.
'Communicating Recursive Objects'.
In *International Workshop on Object-oriented Database Systems*,

Klaus Dittrich and Umeshwar Dayal (eds), pp. 225–226. IEEE Computer Society Press, New York, September 1986.

[Lam89] Winfried Lamersdorf.
'Recursively Defined Objects'.
In *Nested Relations and Complex Objects in Databases*, P.C. Fischer
S. Abiteboul and H.-J. Schek (eds), Lecture Notes in Computer Science, **361**. Springer-Verlag, Berlin, 1989.

[LH89] L.-C. Lie and E. Horowitz.
'Object Database Support for a Software Project Management Environment'.
ACM SIGPLAN Notices, **24**(2): 85–96, February 1989.

[Lin89] Volker Linneman.
'Nested Relations and Recursive Queries'.
In *Nested Relations and Complex Objects in Databases*, P.C. Fischer
S. Abiteboul and H.-J. Schek (eds), Lecture Notes in Computer Science, **361**. Springer-Verlag, Berlin, 1989.

[Lis82] B. Liskov.
'On Linguistic Support for Distributed Programs'.
IEEE Transactions on Software Engineering, **SE-8**(3): 203–218,
May 1982.

[LK86] Peter Lyngbaek and William Kent.
'A Data Modeling Methodology for the Design and Implementation of Information Systems'.
In *International Workshop on Object-oriented Database Systems*,
Klaus Dittrich and Umeshwar Dayal (eds), pp. 6–17. IEEE Computer Society Press, New York, September 1986.

[LL89] Mark Levenne and George Loizou.
'Gamma-acyclic Database Schemes and Nested Relations'.
In *Nested Relations and Complex Objects in Databases*, P.C. Fischer
S. Abiteboul and H.-J. Schek (eds), Lecture Notes in Computer Science, **361**. Springer-Verlag, Berlin, 1989.

[LM88] Q. Li and D. McLeod.
'Supporting Object Flavour Evolution Through Learning in an Object-oriented Database System'.
In *Proceedings of the 2nd International Conference on Expert Database Systems*, April 1988.

[Low87a]   C. Lowe.
'A Shared, Persistent Object Store'.
In *European Conference on Object-oriented Programming*, S. Gjessing and K. Nygaard (eds), Lecture Notes in Computer Science, pp. 390–410. Springer-Verlag, Berlin, August 1987.

[Low87b]   C. Lowe.
'A Shared, Persistent Object Store'.
Technical Report, Department of Computer Science, Queen Mary College, London, 1987.

[LRV88]   C. Lécluse, P. Richard, and F. Velez.
'O_2, An Object-oriented Data Model'.
In *Proceedings of the ACM SIGMOD International Conference on Management of Data*, pp. 425–433, June 1988.

[LS82]   B. Liskov and R. Scheifler.
'Guardians and Actions: Linguistic Support for Robust, Distributed Programs'.
In *Proceedings of the 9th ACM Symposium on Principles of Programming Languages*, pp. 7–19, 1982.

[LSV89]   E. Laenens, F. Staes, and D. Vermeir.
'Browsing a la carte in an Object-oriented Database System'.
The Computer Journal, **32**: 333–340, 1989.

[LTP86]   W.R. LaLonde, D.R. Thomas, and J.R. Pugh.
'An Exemplar Based Smalltalk'.
In *Proceedings of the Object-oriented Programming Systems and Languages Conference*, pp. 322–330, 1986.

[M+88]   R. Morrison *et al.*
'On the Integration of Object-oriented and Process-oriented Computation in a Persistent Environment'.
In *Advances in Object-oriented Database Systems*, K.R. Dittrich (ed.), Lecture Notes in Computer Science, **334**, pp. 334–339. Springer-Verlag, Berlin, 1988.

[Mai86]   David Maier.
'Why Object-oriented Databases Can Succeed Where Others Have Failed'.
In *International Workshop on Object-oriented Database Systems*, Klaus Dittrich and Umeshwar Dayal (eds), p. 227. IEEE Computer Society Press, New York, September 1986.

[Mas88]   Y. Masunaga.
'Object Identity In Omega: An Object-oriented Database System For
Managing Multimedia Data'.
Technical Report, Dept of Computing Science, The University of
Texas, Austin, Texas, May 1988.

[MBH⁺86]   F. Maryanski, J. Bedell, S. Hoelscher, S. Hong, L. McDonald,
J. Peckham, and D. Stock.
'The Data Model Compiler: A Tool for Generating Object-oriented
Database Systems'.
In *International Workshop on Object-oriented Database Systems*,
Klaus Dittrich and Umeshwar Dayal (eds), pp. 73–84. IEEE Com-
puter Society Press, New York, September 1986.

[MCB89]   M.V. Mannino, I.J. Choi, and D.S. Batory.
'An Overview of an Object-oriented Functional Data Language'.
In *Proceedings of the 5th International Conference on Data Engi-
neering*, pp. 18–26, February 1989.

[McL86]   Dennis McLeod.
'Object Management and Sharing in Autonomous, Distributed
Databases'.
In *International Workshop on Object-oriented Database Systems*,
Klaus Dittrich and Umeshwar Dayal (eds), p. 228. IEEE Computer
Society Press, New York, September 1986.

[McL88]   D. McLeod.
'A Learning-based Approach to Metadata Evolution in an Object-
oriented Database'.
In *Advances in Object-oriented Database Systems*, K.R. Dittrich
(ed.), Lecture Notes in Computer Science, **334**, pp. 219–224.
Springer-Verlag, Berlin, 1988.

[MD86]   Frank Manola and Umeshwar Dayal.
'PDM: An Object-oriented Data Model'.
In *International Workshop on Object-oriented Database Systems*,
Klaus Dittrich and Umeshwar Dayal (eds), pp. 18–25. IEEE Com-
puter Society Press, New York, September 1986.

[ME89]   F. Mariategui and M.H. Eich.
'Unit of Consistency in Object-oriented Databases'.
Technical Report 89-CSE-10, Southern Methodist University, Dallas,
Texas, March 1989.

[MER88]   F. Mariategui, M.H. Eich, and S. Rafiqi.
'The Object-oriented Data Model Defined'.
Technical Report 88-CSE-28, Southern Methodist University, Dallas,
Texas, April 1988.

[Mey88]   B. Meyer.
Object-oriented Software Construction.
Prentice-Hall, Englewood Cliffs, N.J., 1988.

[ML87]   T. Merrow and J. Laursen.
'A Pragmatic System for Shared Persistent Objects'.
In *Proceedings of the 2nd ACM Conference on Object-oriented Programming Systems, Languages and Applications*, pp. 103–110, Orlando, Florida, October 1987.

[MO86]   F. Manola and J.A. Orenstein.
'Toward a General Spatial Data Model for an Object-oriented DBMS'.
In *Proceedings of the 12th International Conference on Very Large Databases*, pp. 328–335, Kyoto, August 1986.

[Mos86]   J. Eliot B. Moss.
'Transaction Management for Object-oriented Systems'.
In *International Workshop on Object-oriented Database Systems*, Klaus Dittrich and Umeshwar Dayal (eds), p. 229. IEEE Computer Society Press, New York, September 1986.

[Mos89]   J.E.B. Moss.
'Object-orientation as a Catalyst for Language Database Integration'.
In *Object-oriented Concepts, Databases, and Applications*, W. Kim and F.H. Lochovsky (eds), pp. 583–592. Addison-Wesley, Reading, Mass., 1989.

[MP87]   J. McPherson and H. Pirahesh.
'An Overview of Extensibility in Starburst'.
IEEE Database Engineering, **10**(2): 32–39, June 1987.

[MS86]   David Maier and Jacob Stein.
'Indexing in an Object-oriented DBMS'.
In *International Workshop on Object-oriented Database Systems*, Klaus Dittrich and Umeshwar Dayal (eds), pp. 171–182. IEEE Computer Society Press, New York, September 1986.

[MS87]   D. Maier and J. Stein.
          'Development and Implementation of an Object-oriented DBMS'.
          In *Research Directions in Object-oriented Programming*, Bruce
          Shriver and Peter Wegner (eds), pp. 355–392. MIT Press, Cambridge,
          Mass., 1987.

[MS88]   J.E.B. Moss and S. Sinofsky.
          'Managing Persistent Data with Mneme: Designing a Reliable
          Shared Object Interface'.
          In *Advances in Object-oriented Database Systems*, K.R. Dittrich
          (ed.), Lecture Notes in Computer Science, **334**, pp. 298–316.
          Springer-Verlag, Berlin, 1988.

[MSOP86] D. Maier, J. Stein, A. Otis, and A. Purdy.
          'Development of an Object-oriented DBMS'.
          In *Proceedings of the Object-oriented Programming Systems and
          Languages Conference*, pp. 472–482, July 1986.

[MT86]   S.J. Mullender and A.S. Tannenbaum.
          'The Design of a Capability-based Distributed Operating System'.
          The Computer Journal, **29**(4): 289–299, 1986.

[MZ90]   D. Maier and S.B. Zdonik.
          Readings in Object-oriented Database Systems.
          Morgan Kaufmann, San Mateo, Calif., 1990.

[Nes86]   John R. Nestor.
          'Re-creation and Evolution in a Programming Environment'.
          In *International Workshop on Object-oriented Database Systems*,
          Klaus Dittrich and Umeshwar Dayal (eds), p. 230. IEEE Computer
          Society Press, New York, September 1986.

[NH86]   V. Nguyen and B. Hailpern.
          'A Generalized Object Model'.
          ACM SIGPLAN Notices, **21**(10): 78–87, October 1986.

[Nie89]   O. Nierstrasz.
          'A Survey of Object-oriented Concepts'.
          In *Object-oriented Concepts, Databases, and Applications*, W. Kim
          and F.H. Lochovsky (eds), pp. 3–22. Addison-Wesley, Reading,
          Mass., 1989.

[Nij76]   G.M. Nijssen.
          'Granularity of Locks and Degrees of Consistency in a Shared Data

Base'.
In *Modeling in Data Base Management Systems*. North Holland, Amsterdam, 1976.

[O'B88]   P. O'Brien.
'Common Object-oriented Repository System'.
In *Advances in Object-oriented Database Systems*, K.R. Dittrich (ed.), Lecture Notes in Computer Science, **334**, pp. 329–333. Springer-Verlag, Berlin, 1988.

[OBBT89]   A. Ohori, P. Buneman, and V. Breazu-Tannen.
'Database Programming in Machiavelli—a Polymorphic Language with Static Type Inference'.
In *Proceedings of the 14th Annual ACM Conference on the Management of Data*, pp. 46–57, Portland, Oregon, June 1989.

[OBS86]   P. O'Brien, B. Bullis, and C. Schaffert.
'Persistent and Shared Objects in Trellis/Owl'.
In *Proceedings of the International Workshop on Object-oriented Database Systems*, Klaus Dittrich and Umeshwar Dayal (eds), pp. 113–123. IEEE Computer Society Press, New York, September 1986.

[OHK87]   P. O'Brien, D.C. Halbert, and M.F. Kilian.
'The Trellis Programming Environment'.
In *Proceedings of the 2nd ACM Conference on Object-oriented Programming Systems, Languages and Applications*, pp. 91–102, Orlando, Florida, October 1987.

[Osb86]   Sylvia Osborn.
'Object Modelling'.
In *International Workshop on Object-oriented Database Systems*, Klaus Dittrich and Umeshwar Dayal (eds), p. 231. IEEE Computer Society Press, New York, September 1986.

[Osb87]   S. Osborn.
'Extensible Databases and RAD'.
IEEE Database Engineering, **10**(2): 10–15, 1987.

[Osb88]   S. Osborn.
'Identity, Equality and Query Optimization'.
In *Advances in Object-oriented Database Systems*, K.R. Dittrich (ed.), Lecture Notes in Computer Science, **334**, pp. 346–351. Springer-Verlag, Berlin, 1988.

[OY89]   Z. Meral Ozsoyoglu and Li-Yan Yuan.
'On the Normalization in Nested Relational Databases'.
In *Nested Relations and Complex Objects in Databases*, P.C. Fischer
S. Abiteboul and H.-J. Schek (eds), Lecture Notes in Computer Science, **361**. Springer-Verlag, Berlin, 1989.

[P⁺88]   H.H. Porter *et al.*
'A Distributed Object Server'.
In *Advances in Object-oriented Database Systems*, K.R. Dittrich
(ed.), Lecture Notes in Computer Science, **334**, pp. 43–59. Springer-Verlag, Berlin, 1988.

[Pas89]   W. Paseman.
'Object-oriented Database Panel Position Statement'.
In *Proceedings of the 5th International Conference on Data Engineering*, pp. 419–421, February 1989.

[PD89]   Peter Pistor and Peter Dadam.
'The Advanced Information Management Prototype'.
In *Nested Relations and Complex Objects in Databases*, P.C. Fischer
S. Abiteboul and H.-J. Schek (eds), Lecture Notes in Computer Science, **361**. Springer-Verlag, Berlin, 1989.

[Pet87]   Robert W. Peterson.
'Object-oriented Data Bases'.
AI Expert, pp. 26–31, March 1987.

[Pet88]   E. Petry.
'A Model for an Object Management System for Software Engineering Environments'.
In *Advances in Object-oriented Database Systems*, K.R. Dittrich
(ed.), Lecture Notes in Computer Science, **334**, pp. 262–268.
Springer-Verlag, Berlin, 1988.

[PG88]   N.W. Patton and P.M.D. Gray.
'Identification of Database Objects by Key'.
In *Advances in Object-oriented Database Systems*, K.R. Dittrich
(ed.), Lecture Notes in Computer Science, **334**, pp. 280–285.
Springer-Verlag, Berlin, 1988.

[PJF89]   G. Pathak, J. Joseph, and S. Ford.
'Object Exchange Service for an Object-oriented Database System'.
In *Proceedings of the 5th International Conference on Data Engineering*, pp. 27–34, February 1989.

[PM88]   J. Peckham and F. Maryanski.
'Semantic Data Models'.
ACM Computing Surveys, **20**(3): 153–189, September 1988.

[PPT89]   M. Penedo, E. Ploederer, and I. M. Thomas.
'Object Management Issues for Software Engineering Environments
(Workshop Report)'.
ACM SIGPLAN Notices, **24**(2): 226–234, February 1989.

[PS87]   D.J. Penney and Jacob Stein.
'Class Modification in the GemStone Object-oriented DBMS'.
In *Proceedings of the 2nd ACM Conference on Object-oriented Programming Systems, Languages and Applications*, pp. 111–117, Orlando, Florida, October 1987.

[PV86]   G. Copeland P. Valduriez, S. Khoshafian.
'Implementation Techniques of Complex Objects'.
In *Proceedings of the 12th International Conference on Very Large
Databases*, pp. 101–110, Kyoto, August 1986.

[R⁺88]   S. Rehm *et al.*
'Support for Design Processes in a Structurally Object-oriented
Database System'.
In *Advances in Object-oriented Database Systems*, K.R. Dittrich
(ed.), Lecture Notes in Computer Science, **334**, pp. 80–97. Springer-
Verlag, Berlin, 1988.

[Rao86]   K. V. Rao.
'An Object-oriented Framework for Modelling Design Data'.
In *International Workshop on Object-oriented Database Systems*,
Klaus Dittrich and Umeshwar Dayal (eds), p. 232. IEEE Computer
Society Press, New York, September 1986.

[RC87]   J.E. Richardson and M.J. Carey.
'Programming Constructs for Database System Implementation in
EXODUS'.
In *Proceedings of the 12th Annual ACM Conference on the Manage-
ment of Data*, pp. 208–219, San Francisco, May 1987.

[RMS88]   S. Riegel, F. Mellender, and A. Straw.
'Integration of Database Management with an Object-oriented Pro-
gramming Language'.
In *Advances in Object-oriented Database Systems*, K.R. Dittrich

(ed.), Lecture Notes in Computer Science, **334**, pp. 317–322. Springer-Verlag, Berlin, 1988.

[Rot86]   M. Roth.
Theory of Non-first Normal Form Relational Databases.
PhD thesis, The University of Texas at Austin, 1986.

[Row86]   Lawrence A. Rowe.
'A Shared Object Hierarchy'.
In *International Workshop on Object-oriented Database Systems*, Klaus Dittrich and Umeshwar Dayal (eds), pp. 160–170. IEEE Computer Society Press, New York, September 1986.

[RS85]   R. Ramakrishnan and A. Silbershatz.
'The MR Diagram—A Model for Conceptual Databases Design'.
In *Proceedings of the 11th International Conference on Very Large Databases*, pp. 376–393, Stockholm, 1985.

[RS87]   L.A. Rowe and M.R. Stonebraker.
'The POSTGRES Data Model'.
In *Proceedings of the 13th International Conference on Very Large Databases*, pp. 83–96, 1987.

[SAB+89]   Michel Scholl, Serge Abiteboul, Francois Bancilhon, Nicole Bidoit, Sophie Gamerman, Didier Plateau, Philippe Richard, and Anne Verroust.
'VERSO: A Database Machine Based on Nested Relations'.
In *Nested Relations and Complex Objects in Databases*, P.C. Fischer S. Abiteboul and H.-J. Schek (eds), Lecture Notes in Computer Science, **361**. Springer-Verlag, Berlin, 1989.

[SAH87a]   M. Stonebraker, J. Anton, and E. Hanson.
'Extending a Database System with Procedures'.
ACM Transactions on Database Systems, **12**(3): 350–376, September 1987.

[SAH87b]   M. Stonebraker, J. Anton, and M. Hirohama.
'Extendability in POSTGRES'.
IEEE Database Engineering, **10**(2): 16–23, June 1987.

[SAS89]   P.C. Fischer, S. Abiteboul and H.-J. Schek (eds).
Nested Relations and Complex Objects in Databases.
Lecture Notes in Computer Science, **361**. Springer-Verlag, Berlin, 1989.

[SB85]   M. Stefik and D. Bobrow.
'Object-oriented Programming: Themes and Variations'.
The AI Magazine, pp. 40–62, 1985.

[SB89]   Rudi Studer and Stefan Borner.
'An Approach to Manage Large Inheritance Networks Within a DBS
Supporting Nested Relations'.
In *Nested Relations and Complex Objects in Databases*, P.C. Fischer
S. Abiteboul and H.-J. Schek (eds), Lecture Notes in Computer Sci-
ence, **361**. Springer-Verlag, Berlin, 1989.

[SC89]   E.J. Shekita and M.J. Carey.
'Performance Enhancement Through Replication in an Object-
oriented DBMS'.
In *Proceedings of the 14th Annual ACM Conference on the Management of Data*, pp. 325–336, Portland, Oregon, June 1989.

[SCB+86]   C. Schaffert, T. Cooper, B. Bullis, M. Kilian, and C. Wilpolt.
'An Introduction to Trellis/Owl'.
In *Proceedings of the Object-oriented Programming Systems and
Languages Conference*, pp. 9–16, 1986.

[SCF+86]   P. Schwarz, W. Chang, J.C. Freytag, G. Lohman, J. McPherson,
C. Mohan, and H. Pirahesh.
'Extensibility in the Starburst Database System'.
In *International Workshop on Object-oriented Database Systems*,
Klaus Dittrich and Umeshwar Dayal (eds), pp. 85–92. IEEE Com-
puter Society Press, New York, September 1986.

[SHH87]   M. Stonebraker, E. Hanson, and C. Hong.
'The Design of the POSTGRES Rules System'.
In *Proceedings of the 3rd International Conference on Data Engi-
neering*, pp. 365–374, 1987.

[Shi81]   D.W. Shipman.
'The Functional Data Model and the Language DAPLEX'.
ACM Transactions on Database Systems, 6(1): 140–173, March
1981.

[SKL88]   S.Y.W. Su, V. Krishnamurthy, and H. Lam.
'An Object-oriented Semantic Association Model (OSAM)'.
*AI in Industrial Engineering and Manufacturing: Theoretical Issues
and Applications*, 1988.

[SL88]   H.-J. Schek and R. Lorie.
'On Dynamically Defined Complex Objects and SQL'.
In *Advances in Object-oriented Database Systems*, K.R. Dittrich
(ed.), Lecture Notes in Computer Science, **334**, pp. 323–328.
Springer-Verlag, Berlin, 1988.

[SMR89]   A. Straw, F. Mellender, and S. Riegel.
'Object Management in a Persistent Smalltalk System'.
SOFTWARE—Practice and Experience, **19**(8): 719–37, August
1989.

[Sny87]   A. Snyder.
'Inheritance and the Development of Encapsulated Software Components'.
In *Proceedings of the 20th Annual Hawaii International Conference
on System Sciences*, volume 2, pp. 227–237, 1987.

[SO89]   D. Straube and M. T. Ozsu.
'Queries in Object-oriented Databases: An Equivalent Calculus and
Algebra'.
Technical Report TR 89-16, Department of Computing Science, Uni-
versity of Alberta, April 1989.

[Spa89]   Christine Parent and Stefano Spaccapietra.
'Complex Objects Modelling: An Entity–Relationship Approach'.
In *Nested Relations and Complex Objects in Databases*, P.C. Fischer
S. Abiteboul and H.-J. Schek (eds), Lecture Notes in Computer Sci-
ence, **361**. Springer-Verlag, Berlin, 1989.

[Spo86]   David L. Spooneer.
'An Object-oriented Data Management System for Mechanical
CAD'.
In *International Workshop on Object-oriented Database Systems*,
Klaus Dittrich and Umeshwar Dayal (eds), pp. 233–234. IEEE Com-
puter Society Press, New York, September 1986.

[SR86]   M. Stonebraker and L.A. Rowe.
'The Design of POSTGRES'.
In *Proceedings 1986 of the ACM-SIGMOD Conference on Manage-
ment of Data*, pp. 340–355, Washington DC, May 1986.

[SR87]   M. Stonebraker and L.A. Rowe.
'The POSTGRES Papers'.

Memorandum No. UCB/ERL M86/85, Electronics Research Laboratory, College of Engineering, University of California, Berkeley 94720, June 1987.

[SRHB89]   A.V. Shah, J.E. Rumbaugh, J.H. Hamel, and R.A. Borsari.
'DSM: An Object-relationship Modeling Language'.
In *Proceedings of the 4th ACM Conference on Object-oriented Programming Systems, Languages and Applications*, pp. 191–202, October 1989.

[SS89]   Hans-J. Schek and Marc H. Scholl.
'The Two Roles of Nested Relations in the DASDBS Project'.
In *Nested Relations and Complex Objects in Databases*, P.C. Fischer S. Abiteboul and H.-J. Schek (eds), Lecture Notes in Computer Science, **361**. Springer-Verlag, Berlin, 1989.

[SSS88]   D. Stemple, A. Socorro, and T. Sheard.
'Formalising Objects for Databases using ADABTPL'.
In *Advances in Object-oriented Database Systems*, K.R. Dittrich (ed.), Lecture Notes in Computer Science, **334**, pp. 110–128. Springer-Verlag, Berlin, 1988.

[Sta84]   J.W. Stamos.
'Static Grouping of Small Objects to Enhance Performance of a Paged Virtual Memory'.
ACM Transactions on Computer Systems, **2**(2): 155–180, May 1984.

[Ste88]   Jacob Stein.
'Object-oriented Programming and Databases'.
Dr. Dobbs Journal, **1**(137): 18–34, March 1988.

[Sto86a]   M. Stonebraker.
'Object Management in a Relational Data Base System'.
In *Proceedings of the 31st International IEEE Computer Society Conference (COMPCON 86)*, pp. 336–341, 1986.

[Sto86b]   Michael Stonebraker.
'Object Management in POSTGRES using Procedures'.
In *International Workshop on Object-oriented Database Systems*, Klaus Dittrich and Umeshwar Dayal (eds), pp. 66–72. IEEE Computer Society Press, New York, September 1986.

[Sto87]   M. Stonebraker.
'The Design of the POSTGRES Storage System'.

In *Proceedings of the 13th International Conference on Very Large Databases*, pp. 289–300, 1987.

[Str86a]   R. Strom.
'A Comparison of the Object-oriented and Process Paradigms'.
ACM SIGPLAN Notices, **21**(10): 88–97, October 1986.

[Str86b]   Bjarne Stroustrup.
The C++ Programming Language.
Addison-Wesley, Reading, Mass., March 1986.

[SZ86]   A.H. Skarra and S.B. Zdonik.
'The Management of Changing Types in an Object-oriented Database'.
ACM SIGPLAN Notices, **21**(11): 483–495, November 1986.

[SZ87]   K.E. Smith and S.B. Zdonik.
'Intermedia: A Case Study of the Differences between Relational and Object-oriented Database Systems'.
ACM SIGPLAN Notices, **22**(11): 452–465, November 1987.

[SZ89]   A.H. Skarra and S.B. Zdonik.
'Concurrency Control and Object-oriented Databases'.
In *Object-oriented Concepts, Databases, and Applications*, W. Kim and F.H. Lochovsky (eds), pp. 395–422. Addison-Wesley, Reading, Mass., 1989.

[SZR86]   Andrea H. Skarra, Stanley B. Zdonik, and Stephan P. Reiss.
'An Object Server for an Object-oriented Database System'.
In *International Workshop on Object-oriented Database Systems*, Klaus Dittrich and Umeshwar Dayal (eds), pp. 196–204. IEEE Computer Society Press, New York, September 1986.

[Tak89]   Koichi Takeda.
'On the Uniqueness of Nested Relations'.
In *Nested Relations and Complex Objects in Databases*, P.C. Fischer S. Abiteboul and H.-J. Schek (eds), Lecture Notes in Computer Science, **361**. Springer-Verlag, Berlin, 1989.

[Tha86]   Satish M. Thatte.
'Persistent Memory: A Storage Architecture for Object-oriented Database Systems'.
In *International Workshop on Object-oriented Database Systems*,

Klaus Dittrich and Umeshwar Dayal (eds), pp. 148–159. IEEE Computer Society Press, New York, September 1986.

[Tha87]   Satish M. Thatte.
'Report on the Object-oriented Database Workshop: Implementation Aspects'.
ACM SIGMOD Record, **17**(2): 95–107, Oct. 1987.

[Thu89]   M.B. Thuraisingham.
'Mandatory Security in Object-oriented Database Systems'.
In *Proceedings of the 4th ACM Conference on Object-oriented Programming Systems, Languages and Applications*, pp. 203–10, October 1989.

[TKM86]   O. De Troyer, J. Keustermans, and R. Meersman.
'How Helpful is an Object-oriented Language for an Object-oriented Database Model?'.
In *International Workshop on Object-oriented Database Systems*, Klaus Dittrich and Umeshwar Dayal (eds), pp. 124–132. IEEE Computer Society Press, New York, September 1986.

[TL82]   D. Tsichritzis and F. Lochovsky.
Data Models.
Prentice-Hall, Englewood Cliffs, N.J., 1982.

[TS82]   A. Takeuchi and E. Y. Shapiro.
'Object-oriented Programming in Relational Language'.
Technical report, ICOT Research Center, 1982.

[TYI88]   K. Tanaka, M. Yoshikawa, and K. Ishihara.
'Schema Virtualization in Object-oriented Databases'.
In *Proceedings of the 4th International Conference on Data Engineering*, pp. 23–20, February 1988.

[UD88]   S.D. Urban and L.M.L. Delcambre.
'Constraint Analysis: A Tool for Explaining the Semantics of Complex Objects'.
In *Advances in Object-oriented Database Systems*, K.R. Dittrich (ed.), Lecture Notes in Computer Science, **334**, pp. 156–161. Springer-Verlag, Berlin, 1988.

[UD89]   S.D. Urban and L.M.L. Delcambre.
'Constraint Analysis for Specifying Perspectives of Class Objects'.

In *Proceedings of the 5th International Conference on Data Engineering*, pp. 10–17, February 1989.

[Ull82] J.D. Ullman.
Principles of Database Systems.
Computer Science Press, Rockville, Maryland, 1982.

[Ull87] J.D. Ullman.
'Database Theory: Past and Future'.
In *Proceedings of the 6th ACM SIGACT-SIGMOD Symposium on the Principles of Database Systems*, pp. 1–10, March 1987.

[Ull89] J.D. Ullman.
Principles of Database and Knowledge-base Systems, volume 1.
Computer Science Press, Rockville, Maryland, 1989.

[VD88] P. Valduriez and S. Danforth.
'Query Optimization in FAD, a Database Programming Language'.
Technical Report ACA-ST-316-88, Microelectronics and Computer Technology Corporation, 1988.

[VPF89] S.T. Vinter, N. Phadnis, and R. Floyd.
'Distributed Query Processing in CRONUS'.
In *Proceedings of the 9th International Conference on Distributed Computing Systems*, pp. 414–422, June 1989.

[W+89] S.P. Weiser *et al.*
'OZ+: An Object-oriented Database System'.
In *Object-oriented Concepts, Databases, and Applications*, W. Kim and F.H. Lochovsky (eds), pp. 309–339. Addison-Wesley, Reading, Mass., 1989.

[Weg86] P. Wegner.
'Classification in Object-oriented Systems'.
ACM SIGPLAN Notices, **21**(10): 173–182, October 1986.

[Weg87] P. Wegner.
'Dimensions of Object-based Language Design'.
In *Proceedings of the 2nd ACM Conference on Object-oriented Programming Systems, Languages and Applications*, pp. 168–182, Orlando, Florida, October 1987.

[Wha89] K.Y. Whang.
'A Seamless Integration in Object-oriented Database Systems'.

In *Proceedings of the 5th International Conference on Data Engineering*, pp. 675–676, February 1989.

[Wie86a]   Douglas Wiebe.
'A Distributed Repository for Immutable Persistent Objects'.
ACM SIGPLAN Notices, **21**(11): 453–465, November 1986.

[Wie86b]   Gio Wiederhold.
'Views, Objects, and Databases'.
IEEE Computer, **19**(12): 37–44, December 1986.

[Wil88]   W. Wilkes.
'Instance Inheritance Mechanisms for Object-oriented Databases'.
In *Advances in Object-oriented Database Systems*, K.R. Dittrich (ed.), Lecture Notes in Computer Science, **334**, pp. 274–279. Springer-Verlag, Berlin, 1988.

[WK87]   D. Woelk and W. Kim.
'An Extensible Framework for Multimedia Information management'.
IEEE Database Engineering, **10**(2): 55–61, 1987.

[WKL86]   D. Woelk, W. Kim, and W. Luther.
'An Object-oriented Approach to Multimedia Databases'.
ACM SIGPLAN Notices, **15**(2): 311–325, June 1986.

[WL88]   P. Van Der Wolf and T. Van Leuken.
'Object Type Oriented Data Modelling for VLSI Data Management'.
In *Proceedings 25th ACM/IEEE Design Automation Conference*, pp. 351–356, 1988.

[YI85]   Haruo Yokota and Hidenori Itoh.
'A Model and an Architecture for a Relational Knowledge Base'.
Technical Report TR-141, ICOT Research Center, November 1985.

[ZAKB+86]   Carlo Zaniolo, Hassan Ait-Kaci, David Beech, Stephanie Cammarata, Larry Kerschberg, and David Maier.
'Object-oriented Database Systems and Knowledge Systems'.
In *Expert Database Systems; Proceedings From the First International Workshop*, Larry Kerschberg (ed.), pp. 49–65. Benjamin/Cummings, Reading, Mass., 1986.

[Zan85]   C. Zaniolo.
'The Representation and Deductive Retrieval of Complex Objects'.

In *Proceedings of the 11th International Conference on Very Large Databases*, pp. 458–469, Stockholm, 1985.

[Zdo86]   S. Zdonik.
'Why Properties are Objects or Some Refinements of "is-a" '.
In *ACM/IEEE Fall Joint Computer Conference*, pp. 41–47, November 1986.

[Zdo88]   S.B. Zdonik.
'Data Abstraction and Query Optimization'.
In *Advances in Object-oriented Database Systems*, K.R. Dittrich (ed.), Lecture Notes in Computer Science, **334**, pp. 368–373. Springer-Verlag, Berlin, 1988.

[ZR88]   Liping Zhao and S.A. Roberts.
'An Object-oriented Model for Database Modelling, Implementation and Access'.
BCS Computer Journal, **31**(2): 116–124, April 1988.

[ZSGC86]   C. Zaroliagis, P. Soupos, S. Goutas, and D. Christodoulakis.
'The Graspin DB—A Syntax Directed, Language Independent Software Engineering Database'.
In *International Workshop on Object-oriented Database Systems*, Klaus Dittrich and Umeshwar Dayal (eds), p. 235. IEEE Computer Society Press, New York, September 1986.

[ZW85]   Stanley B. Zdonik and Peter Wegner.
'Language and Methodology for Object-oriented Database Environments'.
Technical Report, Brown University, Dept of Computer Science, Providence R.I. USA, November 1985.

INDEX